SOCIAL WORK PRACTICE WITH LOW-INCOME, URBAN, AFRICAN-AMERICAN FAMILIES

Front cover:
Illustration by Diane Kramer

SOCIAL WORK PRACTICE WITH LOW-INCOME, URBAN, AFRICAN-AMERICAN FAMILIES

Melvyn Raider
and
Mary Beth Pauline-Morand

The Edwin Mellen Press
Lewiston•Queenston•Lampeter

Library of Congress Cataloging-in-Publication Data

Social work practice with low-income, urban, African-American families
/ Melvyn Raider and Mary Beth Pauline-Morand.
    p. cm.
Includes bibliographical references and index.
ISBN 0-7734-8306-3
    1. Social work with Afro-Americans.   2. Afro-American families-
-Services for. 3. Urban poor--Services for--United States.
I. Raider, Melvyn.   II. Pauline-Morand, Mary Beth.
HV3181.S623   1998
362.84' 96073--DC21

98-8627
CIP

A CIP catalog record for this book is available from the British Library.

Copyright © 1998   Melvyn Raider and Mary Beth Pauline-Morand

All rights reserved. For information contact

The Edwin Mellen Press
Box 450
Lewiston, New York
USA 14092-0450

The Edwin Mellen Press
Box 67
Queenston, Ontario
CANADA L0S 1L0

The Edwin Mellen Press, Ltd.
Lampeter, Ceredigion, Wales
UNITED KINGDOM SA48 8LT

Printed in the United States of America

Dedication

To Eileen and John for their love and support throughout our work on this project.

Contents

Preface
Social Work Practice with Low-Income, Urban African-American Families
Raider and Pauline-Morand

The practice of social work is a most complex professional enterprise. The skillful practitioner is required to be knowledgeable about the science of human behavior, to possess a thorough understanding of helping relationships, to be familiar with the impact of economics and social class on human and social functioning, and to have a clear understanding of the role of culture in shaping peoples' perspective, identity, and self-concept. The complexity of the enterprise, however, does not end here. The skilled practitioner must also have a more than passing command of dynamics of family relations, social status, and human adaptation. With this knowledge in hand, one is equipped with the basics needed to offer competent service to one's clientele- save for one additional element. To the above, must be added a sensitive appreciation and knowledge of racial and ethnic factors in shaping the client's perception, behavior, coping, and willingness to change.

Acquiring the knowledge and skill catalog, above would pose no small challenge even if it were readily accessible. But scattering among scores of books and articles, often incompletely conceptualized, and presented with insufficient attention to strategies for intervention, acquiring this knowledge becomes an almost monumental task. Thus, even the most diligent seeker of this information finds the quest fruitless.

The writers of this book were acutely aware of the need for a framework to address the absence of information on service to low-income, urban, African-American families. Their interest in the subject grew out of involvement in a project designed to deliver mental health services to selected public schools in the city of Detroit. They quickly discovered that the social workers, regardless of

i

race, were seriously challenged by the task of providing services to low-income, African-American families. How to equip the social workers with the tools to meet the challenges before them became the central focus of their work.

In many ways, their search was comparable to that of many writers who preceded them. The question they asked had been raised by others whose work yielded helpful ideas and analysis of the literature to identify critical elements of a practice model for working with this population. In doing so, the writers have developed a systematic approach grounded in existing knowledge and validated by the scientific method.

The outcome of this effort is an approach which is consistent with the perspective of many of the classic works as wells as more recent treatises on services to low-income, urban African-American families. This book represents a certain continuity in the scholarship of its predecessors adding to earlier insights the dimension of field testing. For example, Andrew Billingsley's (1968) observations on the important role played by extended family members is reflected in this model. Robert Hill's (1971, 1978) work on the strengths of Black families finds continued validation in this empirical analysis, and Boyd-Franklin's (1990) practice wisdom regarding the significance of the client's perspective finds a central place in the theoretical underpinnings of this book.

The reader will find in this book a perspective grounded in practice observations, linked to the best in the literature, and validated through empirical research. Familiar prescriptions for interventions are offered with a foundation which should give practitioners greater confidence and teachers and students will find the concepts offered to have a firmer theoretical underpinning. Thus, the work moves practice wisdom toward the surer footing of practice knowledge.

Leon W. Chestnag, Ph.D.
Wayne State University
Detroit, MI

ii

Chapter I: Introduction

The authors conceived the notion of developing a model for social workers to practice with low-income African-American families as an outgrowth of their evaluation research on school-based mental health programs. These programs located in inner-city Detroit Schools primarily served low income African-American families. Findings of process evaluation research studies indicated that parents of the children receiving school-based services perceived that there was little communication between social workers and themselves. Further, parents did not feel sufficiently involved in their child's treatment. Social workers in these programs perceived parents as inaccessible, difficult to engage and generally indifferent to being involved in their children's treatment. In spite of the fact that social workers acknowledged the necessity to involve parents and, if necessary, provide family therapy, few parents visited the schools for this purpose and even fewer home visits took place. Consequently, it became obvious that social workers needed additional training to engage parents and bring them into the treatment process. The Model of Social Work Practice with low income, urban, African-American families was developed to train these social workers and ultimately to improve their effectiveness with this population.

The task of developing such a social work practice model was indeed challenging. There has been a great deal written about African-American culture and counseling approaches. Much of this is based upon experiential and anecdotal information. What was needed was to compress this immense volume of literature into a useable format and to develop knowledge and treatment components of a concise, practical intervention model. Further, it was necessary to go beyond

1

anecdotal and experiential sources of knowledge to validate the components of the model. In order to empirically validate the model, qualitative and quantitative research was conducted with the workers who were actually providing services to low-income African-American families.

To provide structure to this task, Edwin Thomas' Developmental Research approach was used as a working methodology for the process of crafting the practice model. Thomas' approach was accepted since it provided a systematic methodology for assessing the state of existing knowledge, validating that knowledge and developing an innovative practice paradigm.

The Design & Development Model of Practice Research

Phase one and two of the design and development model of Practice Research served as a beginning framework for the development of our Model of Social Work Practice with Low-income, Urban, African-American Families. This approach was introduced by Edwin Thomas, among others, almost twenty years ago (Thomas '78). Unlike traditional research methods which seek to contribute to our knowledge base, Design & Development research seeks to develop new practice approaches or innovations. Thomas refers to his Design and Development approach as the Developmental Research Approach to D&D (Thomas 1992). For Thomas "the outcomes of developmental research are products that are the technical means of achieving social work and social welfare objectives" (Thomas, 1992 p. 73). The four major phases of the approach are: analysis of existing knowledge and the state of the art in the area in which the innovation is to take place; design of the intervention approach; development of the implementation plan; and evaluation of the effectiveness of the intervention (Thomas, 1992 p. 74). The analysis and design of the Developmental model involved analysis of relevant literature and the state of existing interventions. It also included empirical data gathering in order to determine the most appropriate selection of information and data sources to be included in the Model. The design phase of model construction involved exploration of new interventions based upon the analysis of relevant

2

information and empirical data gathering.

Analysis of relevant information and the status of existing interventions

A literature review was conducted which examined the characteristics and history of African-American families; barriers to services, and practice approaches which have been proposed to be helpful with African-American families. A later task of the analysis phase of the Developmental Research Approach was the selection of information sources and the gathering and processing of information necessary to refine the intervention model.

In order to develop a model that was both grounded in theory as well as consistent with current social work practice, a qualitative and quantitative exploratory survey of service providers in agencies serving low-income, urban, African-American families was implemented and analyzed. A purposive sample of twenty-five respondents from ten agencies was obtained. Three agencies were residential programs which focused on child and family services, one was a school outreach program serving families, five of them were school based mental health programs, and one was a program which provided medical social work and support services to families.

Instrument Development:

Based on the information obtained in the literature review, instruments were developed. Using these instruments, researchers sought to gather further information regarding the five potential model components selected as a result of the literature review. The instruments were also designed to empirically validate the intervention techniques postulated as helpful to low-income, urban, African-American families.

The first instrument developed was a three-part questionnaire. The first part of the questionnaire was composed of open-ended questions. The questionnaire was constructed to determine how the families were most often referred; services most often used by African-Americans in the respondent's program; strategies and techniques used by the participant to help the families; and

3

the worker's level of experience with the target population. Participants in the survey were also asked to describe a successful as well as an unsuccessful intervention with low-income, urban, African-American families.

Information obtained from the literature review suggested that it was important for workers who serve low-income, urban, African-American families to have knowledge of African-Americans culture. Consequently, twenty-six Likert Scale items focused on history and culture; self-esteem; support from extended family and the community; spirituality and religion; safety issues and living conditions; gender roles; and the roles of grandparents. The same format was used to focus on practice principles. Nineteen Likert Scale items on the questionnaire gathered data regarding family workers' perceptions and use various treatment techniques for service delivery to low-income, urban, African American families. Techniques examined in this component of the questionnaire included: the role of extended families in services; the role of religion, spirituality and the church community in service provision; and communication techniques to overcome communication and language barriers. The entire questionnaire was reviewed by a sample of workers serving low income urban African-American families to establish face validity.

The study sample was composed of 11 school-based mental health workers from the Detroit Compact Child and Family Program, and 14 social workers or therapists from six other programs. These included three residential programs which focused on child and family services; one school outreach program which focused on child and family services; and one program based in a medical agency which provided medical social work and support services to families. From these six outside agencies, two respondents were second year Master of Social Work students who volunteered to participate in the study after an announcement was made in their social work class regarding this study. The sample was a convenience sample, meaning that the agencies were selected for participation based on their degree of experience with the identified population and their

4

willingness to participate in the research.

Data Collection:

Respondents completed the three-part questionnaire in the presence of the researcher, the 20-minute face-to-face interview followed a few minutes after completion. Respondents who completed the questionnaire independently returned the questionnaire to the interviewer a few minutes before the face-to-face interview. To complete interviews, the researcher visited each respondent's workplace. Before conducting the interview, the researcher reviewed each participant's questionnaire, and marked areas for in depth exploration. In addition to a list of standard questions asked, the interviewer tailored each interview according to the participant's responses. For example, if a respondent gave an answer to an open-ended question, stating that he/she had 5 years experience with the target population in a hospital setting; and five years experience in a outreach setting, the interviewer might find it useful to ask the participant differences and similarities in service delivery and how the target population responded to services in each setting. At the end of each interview, participants were asked to give the interviewer feedback regarding the use of the instrument and the study itself.

Data Analysis: Open-ended Questions

Quantitative data gathered from the questionnaire was analyzed using SPSS for Windows, version 6.0. Data collected from the interviews and the open-ended portion of the questionnaire was qualitatively analyzed using the Hyperresearch Program, version 2.0. The first part of the questionnaire contained eight open-ended questions formulated to obtain information regarding respondents' experience and practice approaches in work with the target population. Findings for this part of the questionnaire suggested that 100% of the participants had experience with low-income, urban, African-American families in various settings. The percentages of participants (for all participants) according to work settings were as follows: residential, 17.7%; school/school-based, 14.5%; outpatient clinics, 9.6%; domestic violence, homeless, or crisis shelters, 8.1%;

community mental health agencies and vocational settings, 6.45% each: outreach, foster care and home-based programs, 4.8% each: counseling and other social work agencies, 3.2% each; and recreational, hospital, long term health-related; advocacy, Department of Social services, and substance abuse, 1.6% each.

Respondents reported that many of the families with whom they currently worked were low-income, urban, African-American families: 87.5% of the respondents reported that at least 40% of the families receiving services in their agency were low-income, urban African-American families; 62.5% of those surveyed reported that at least 80% of the families who receive services at their agency were low-income, urban, African-American families; 45.8% of the respondents reported that 90% or more of the families receiving services at their agencies are low-income, urban, African-American families; and 20.8% of the respondents reported that 100% of the families at their agencies were low-income, urban, African-American families.

With regard to services often provided to low-income African-American families, concrete services appeared most often, accounting for 30.4% of the service named. Responses grouped under the category of concrete services included services which help the families gain access to food, clothing, housing and medical needs. Next in order of frequency of services provided was family therapy which made up 16% of the responses.

Support services and individual therapy each accounted for 7.1% of the services listed. Services provided by the Department of Social Services were listed in 5.4% of the responses. Outpatient services, community-based programs, medical and health services, substance abuse services, follow-up care, community mental health services, and other social work services each accounted for 3.6% of the services listed. Other services listed each making up 1.8% of the responses were: psychiatric, residential, recreational, parenting education and group therapy services.

Respondents' specification of the issues most frequently brought up in

6

family therapy with low-income, urban, African-American families were as follows: food, housing, clothing and medical, 22.3%; employment, 9.6%; finding needed resources, 8.5%; and threat of crime, 8.5%. All of these may be considered concrete needs and total 48.9% of the responses listed. These responses were followed by mental health issues and parenting skills which were each listed in 6.4% of the responses. Other issues listed and their corresponding percentages are as follows: behavior problems, missed appointments, difficult therapy issues, and substance abuse, 5.3% each; family relationships, 4.3%; physical/sexual abuse, recreational and community support and education, 3.2% each; single parenting, 2.1% and self-esteem, 1.1%.

Of the five agencies which participated in this study which were Detroit Compact School-Based Programs, teachers (15%) and other school staff (32.5%) accounted for 47.5% of the referrals listed by Detroit-Compact respondents. Sources of referral for the other six agencies are described in Table 1.

Table 1.

Referral Source	Occurrence
Courts	22.5%
Department of Social Services	19.4%
Self-referred	9.7%
Hospitals	9.7%
Other school staff	6.5%
Teachers	6.5%
Protective services	6.5%
Word of mouth	6.5%
Foster Care	6.5%
Counselors	3.2%
Mental Health Clinics	3.2%

Table 2. Strategies & Techniques	Occurrence
Behavior Modification	19.7%
Empowerment	12.9%
Showing Respect	9.8%
Cognitive Therapy	8.1%
Brief Crisis Intervention	8.1%
Individual Therapy	4.8%
Client-Centered Therapy	4.8%
Active Listening	3.2%
Building Rapport	3.2%
Family Systems Techniques	3.2%
Group Therapy	3.2%
Education	3.2%
Incorporating Spirituality	3.2%
Gestalt Techniques	3.2%
Providing Concrete Services	1.6%
Play Therapy	1.6%
Case Management	1.6%
Use of Genograms	1.6%
Eclectic	1.6%
Restructuring Family Relationships	1.6%

9

The workers surveyed were asked to rank, according to their perception of effectiveness, strategies and techniques they used to work with low-income, urban, African-American families. In response, participants named a wide variety of strategies and techniques which were grouped according to 20 categories. The categories and corresponding occurrence rates are displayed in Table 2.

Respondents were asked if they identified with a particular theoretical framework in their work with the low-income, urban, African-American families. In response, 40% of the workers surveyed reported that they used many theoretical frameworks in their work with this group. Twenty percent stated that they identified with the Structural Family Therapy model. Other participants reported that they identified with Cognitive or Family Systems models; a smaller percentage of respondents reported that they identified with brief therapy; client-centered therapy; or multisystemic models at a rate of 3.3% each. Respondents were also asked to identify a theoretical framework most often used at their particular agencies. For the most part, respondents seemed reluctant to name any particular model as 44% of those surveyed reported that they did not know which family practice model was most often utilized in the services provided at their agency. Approximately 16% of all respondents named the Structural Family Therapy; 8% named the Family System model; and 4% identified an intensive family therapy model, an eclectic approach, a strategic model or a multi-systemic model.

The last open-ended question asked participants to describe a case involving work with urban, low-income African-American families which they felt was successful as well as a case which they felt was unsuccessful. Cases involving the lack of parenting skills was named in 53% of the unsuccessful cases described and in 50% of the successful cases. The families' lack of concrete needs was named in 33% of the successful cases described and in 35.5% of the unsuccessful cases. Issues related to violence and the need for safety were named 35.5% of the time in descriptions of unsuccessful cases and these issues were reported less

10

often in cases described as successful. Other issues identified in unsuccessful cases were substance abuse, trauma, and single parenting which together were identified 29.4% of the time. Physical and sexual abuse was named in 23.5% of the unsuccessful cases as well.

Data Analysis: Closed Ended Questionnaire Items

Findings indicated that the presence of extended family was important for the target population as 40% of those surveyed specified that "many" or "most" of the target families whom they served received help and emotional support from extended family. Respondents also reported that 80% of these families regarded their extended family as important. Forty-eight percent of the respondents surveyed reported that grandparents serve as primary care givers in "many" or "most" cases. Furthermore, respondents indicated that African-American grandparents play strong roles in their families in "many" or "most" of the families whom they worked with. Fifty-six percent of the respondents indicated in the families with whom they work few parents are married; and 92% of the these professionals reported that "many" or "most" of these African-American households are female headed.

Support from church communities was not rated as highly as was expected. From the sample group, less than half of those surveyed reported that "many" or "most" of these low-income, urban, African-American families received support from church communities. Another important characteristic we identified was regarding safety issues. Over half of the respondents (52%) reported that "few" of the low-income, urban, African-American families with whom they work live in safe areas. These results seem consistent with another finding in this questionnaire in which 92% of the participants reported that "many" or "most" of the target families they worked with have experienced trauma.

Information on practice approaches indicated 58.4% of those surveyed thought that "many" or "most" of the target families found problem-solving interventions beneficial; and 54% of the participants thought that positive change

11

for the families was most likely to occur when the worker used a directive approach. Eighty-eight percent of the respondents indicated that it was critical to gain the trust of African-American family leaders. Sixty-eight percent of the respondents reported that "few" or "some" of the families with whom they worked were resistant to their interventions. Eight-eight percent of those surveyed reported that "many" or "most" of the target families with whom they worked lacked concrete resources; while 68% reported that many or most of these families struggle to meet basic survival needs. Sixty percent of these respondents also reported that "many" or "most" of the parents in these families needed help with establishing parenting boundaries. It was reported that by 76% of those surveyed that "many" or "most" of the parents they worked with needed information regarding parental rights, employment, and access to concrete resources.

Survey research findings together with extensive review of literature concerning practice with poor African-American families facilitated the articulation of the five framework components which constitute a knowledge base necessary for professionals who intend to serve low-income, urban, African-American families. These are: 1) strength/resilience; 2) gender roles; 3) extended family; 4) Black Church, religion and spirituality; and 5) trauma, grief and loss. Similarly, a number of intervention strategies were articulated which are intended for professionals who intend to intervene or help low-income African-American families to more effectively function in their social environments.

Chapter II: Framework Components for Work with Low-income, Urban, African-American Families

Knowledge Framework Component 1: Strength/Resilience

Both our research as well as practice literature supports the view that work with low-income, urban , African-American families is best approached with the use of the strength/resiliency perspective. Social workers who work from this perspective recognize that all families have strengths, and begin family assessments by identifying positive ways that families attempt to deal with problems. Throughout the therapeutic process, the worker can build on and further develop these strengths. As the process unfolds, new strengths will be revealed, and the worker assists family members in the achievement of their identified goals. Thus, the identification and building of family strengths acts as a tool for families' achievement of success and independence.

In this chapter, we will discuss what is meant by the strengths/resiliency perspective; demonstrate how this perspective is practiced; and give examples of programs which have effectively implemented this approach. We will then show how this perspective specifically applies to low-income, urban, African-American families by providing case illustration examples of use of the strength/resiliency perspective with African-American families. W. Patrick Sullivan describes this perspective as the idea that "mentally challenged people have strengths and abilities that can be tapped to foster their continued integration in community settings (1991)". As it is incorporated into our model, the strengths/resiliency perspective means that families/individuals have strengths which have helped them to survive and function in the midst of various problems and difficulties. To understand the

13

strengths/resiliency perspective, one must first examine the problems facing families as well as individuals in the family. Then, one asks the question "What did the family/individual do in order to cope with these problems, and thus, function and survive in the community?" The goal here is to identify positive ways each family/individual has attempted to deal with problems, and then build on these strengths. This perspective has also been identified as a non-deficit perspective (Daly, Jennings, Beckett, and Leashore, 1995). Although there has been much discussion about this perspective, little has been written about how one goes about identifying strengths, and there is even less information regarding how this perspective is to be introduced to professional training (Kaplan & Girard, 1994).

One reason for such scarcity is that the model avoids emphasizing a family's deficits, and it focuses on the family's potential capabilities. Traditional treatment approaches tend to identify what is wrong with individuals, and work to help them to correct or accept such limitations or pathologies (Kaplan & Girard, 1994). The strengths/resiliency perspective differs from such approaches as it allows social workers to move beyond the deficit-focused model of assessment and into a growth-development model, identifying what is right in families rather than simply examining problems (Sallee & Manns, 1991). This perspective is based on the belief that all families have a unique set of strengths, and the challenge for workers is to acknowledge and appreciate family strengths so that families may begin to believe in their capacity to help themselves (Massachusetts Department of Social Services, 1993). It is important to recognize that strengths and resiliency are separate, yet related terms. For our purposes, strengths represent the actual attributes which the families and individuals possess. To find these strengths, we must examine each family's unique resilience. We must work with families to examine the obstacles they have overcome and those obstacles which they currently face. Once we have worked with the families to identify obstacles, we ask, "What has made this family resilient? What has made it possible for them to overcome such obstacles? How did the family survive such obstacles? and, How

14

is the family coping and surviving now?" The answers to these questions provides the worker with a set of strengths on which to build.

Learning to approach family therapy from a strengths perspective is the first essential step toward the implementation and practice of the strengths/resiliency perspective. This first step is the most important and perhaps the most difficult. The difficulty here may lie primarily in the challenge of beginning to think outside of the traditional and often stereotypical paradigms which society perpetuates. Often, workers may find it difficult to assess the strengths of low-income, urban, African-American families in settings that focus primarily on deficits and problems. Although building on family strengths is important, families enter into therapy because they are dealing with problems. Consequently, family strengths which are present may not be evident. Thus, workers need to integrate approaches in which one explores problems as well as family strengths.

A number of social programs have utilized the strengths/resiliency approach in their work with families. A noteworthy example is family preservation programs. Such programs which aim to keep children at home with their families, seem to have successfully integrated acknowledgment of strengths while also showing awareness of family problems (Kinney, Haapala, & Booth, 1991). Both of these strategies are essential and complimentary to the assessment process and to family services provided to low-income, urban, African-American families. The assessment approach used in family preservation programs operates from three premises. According to the first premise, problem definitions are to be perceived as constructs in order to make them more relevant to the successful resolution of problems. The second premise addresses the needs of families in crisis and careful consideration of challenges present during the assessment phase. It should be noted that crises often prompt reluctant families into services. At this time the families may feel unsafe or out of control and they may want to give up before even beginning the problem-solving process. The third premise asserts that

15

assessments should include descriptions of both strengths and problems, advocating awareness of potential capacities. This premise also indicates that the manner in which one describes strengths and problems can either help of hinder the family's problem-solving process (Kinney, Haapala, & Booth, 1991, p.79).

The preceding premises serve as the groundwork for the assessment framework implemented in the Homebuilders model. The following strategies and techniques which will be identified will also prove beneficial to low-income, urban, African-American families in therapy. When applying the first premise which involves viewing problems as constructs, the family worker should use assessment as a means of organizing information in order to bring about change (Kinney, Haapala & Booth, 1991). When gathering information, Kinney, Haapala & Booth (1991) warn family workers to refrain from confusing assessments as the "ultimate truth". Here it is essential to remember that families and their definitions of problems change rapidly, especially if the family is in crisis. Thus, truth is relative. In addition, workers who serve low-income, urban, African-American families will find it crucial to work from the perspective that the information presented by the family is culturally relative (Boyd-Franklin, 1990). This means that the worker should examine cultural significance of all behavior and situations before labeling such occurrences with diagnostic terms which denote disorders or deficits.

In light of the second premise which implies that situations of families in crisis change quickly, it is important for workers to make multiple assessments and to allow sufficient time for these assessments to take place. However, one may feel rushed in the initial assessment process. Although many agencies impose time limitations on workers who serve families, it is important for workers to spend enough time on the initial assessment so that the process itself is not completed prematurely. When conducting the initial assessment, it is important for workers to remember that assessment is never "done" (Kinney, Haapala & Booth, 1991). Homebuilders' workers have found that if adequate time is spent with families, during the assessment phase, and workers are able to understand all that families

16

want them to comprehend, future interventions are more likely to go smoothly. Abbreviating this phase may cause workers to make recommendations about problems which are a low priority for the family. Workers may suggest that the families try things they have already tried or push them to work on irrelevant issues.

Just as workers strive to gain the family's trust, workers must also learn to trust the family. One basic way of doing this is for workers to trust that the family members have the most information about their situation. Family workers often place undue importance on previous records which may be of limited value if those who prepared the records have not been able to spend a great deal of time with the family or if workers have not had the opportunity to view family members in their natural environments (Kinney, Haapala & Booth, 1991).

Active listening and finding ways to hear the "whole story" from each family member's point of view is suggested. To accomplish this, it is critical that extended family and informal family be involved in the assessment interviews. It may also be necessary to conduct the assessment in the family's home to involve the whole family. Once the family's story has been heard, workers need to validate their understanding of the story with family members to ensure that they have heard and understood their story correctly. Workers need to do this as frequently as necessary as well as when assessments are updated.

The Strengths/Resiliency Perspective as Applied to Work with Low-Income, Urban, African-American families

It is necessary to begin our explanation of the five framework components by focusing on the strengths/resiliency perspective since exploration and discussion of the other four components will further demonstrate the resilience and strengths one may identify in African-American families. Let us illustrate the strength/resiliency perspective utilizing the other four framework components (these will be discussed in greater detail in upcoming sections) to illustrate examples of resilience and strengths in African-American families. For African-

American families, the flexibility of male and female roles has been used as a means of coping with oppression (McGoldrick, Pearce & Giordano, 1982). However, such coping mechanisms have often been viewed as deficits because they are not consistent with traditional societal norms. In this way, professionals who work with low-income African-American families are challenged to think beyond traditional paradigms. For example, African-American women whose male spouses are not present in the home often take on many roles in caring for their families. If we are thinking from a traditional perspective, we may view the absence of a male figure in the home as a deficit. However, if we think from the perspective strength and resiliency, we will look at these women as energetic, resourceful women who have taken on various roles in order to care for their families.

An example of African-American families' strength and resilience may be demonstrated in how the family utilizes extended family and community supports to cope with domestic violence. Among significant traumas which occur in the home, domestic violence is of obvious importance. Existing research indicates that the way African-American women cope with domestic violence differs from that of Caucasian women (Coley & Beckett, 1988). African-American women who have experienced domestic violence rely more heavily on extended family and social supports. This type of support is consistent with the African-American value of the extended family and caring for the well-being of others in the community. In addition, support systems such as extended family, the presence of a non-nuclear family member in the home, or long-time residence in the neighborhood seemed to reduce the number of spousal assaults among African-Americans (Coley & Beckett, 1988).

For African-American women, perceptions of the battering experience also differ from those of Caucasian women (Beckett & Coley, 1987; Richie, 1981; & Vontress, 1973). African-American women are more likely to consider physical abuse as related to sexual and racial oppression. Thus, these women are unlikely to see the violence in individual or family power terms. In contrast to the beliefs of Caucasian women, African-American women are likely to view battering as displacement of the African-American male's displaced anger and aggression which they perceive as his responses to economic and social role conflicts. The African-American Community often provides a supportive structure for African-American families who have struggled with domestic violence. Family, neighbors, and other members of the community often provide advice, counseling, shelter and support in order to ease family problems.

Historically, African-Americans have demonstrated the importance of kinship bonds (McGoldrick, et al., 1991). Contrary to the individualistic theme reflected by Descartes, "I think therefore, I am," Africans valued the collective statement, "We are, therefore, I am," (McGoldrick, et al., 1991, p. 557). Today's African-American family unit continues to value extended family which may include friends, grandparents, cousins, neighbors, and co-workers (McAdoo, 1995). According to McGoldrick, one may come to recognize that African-American families' wealth lies not in their bank account, but in the support available to them from a host of extended family members (McGoldrick, et al., 1991). It is important to get past the idea that family composition is only determined by marriage or bloodlines.

To understand how many African-American families are structured, another strength of African-American families is the adaptability of family roles (Hill, 1971). Many African-American families have participated in informal adoptions. The practice may be seen in two and three generational homes in which family members or friends have taken on the responsibility of caring for a loved one's children because the biological parent is emotionally, physically or financially unable to do so. In most cases, there are no papers to show legal guardianship. To see the strength in informal adoption, social workers and family therapists need to overlook the absence of the legal guardianship papers, and consider the commitment to the biological parent who does not want to lose his/her children.

19

These parents hope to provide for their children in the future, and they feel more safe and confident knowing that their children are being cared for by "family" rather than placed in the "system". For the most part, the process of informal adoption is regarded neither as neglect nor as a rejection and the length of these arrangements is often not predetermined. Arrangements may be planned as temporary although they may become permanent due to the development of emotional bonds (McGoldrick, et al., 1991).

Another strength which has historically been present in African-American families is their use of religion and spirituality to cope with oppression. A great deal of literature identifies religion and spirituality as a source of resilience and strength among African-American families (Daly, Jennings, Beckett and Leashore, 1995; Raider, 1992). Despite numerous struggles, African-American religious institutions have served families in many ways (Hill, 1978; Bagley & Thomas, E.J., "Generating Innovation in Social Work: The paradigm of development research " Journal of Social Science Research, (2) 1978.)

When exploring the final framework component, trauma, grief, and loss, strength may be found in the families coping skills which are used to overcome the effects of various traumatic events. It is important for social workers to perceive these families as survivors as they have survived trauma's such as the murder of a loved one; the destruction of their home; separation from their children or other relatives; or the various types of criminal assaults.

Thus far, we have discussed general examples of strengths which have existed or may exist for African-American families with regard to each of the framework components. It is also important to expand on these so that social workers may integrate the strength/resiliency perspective into practice. The case illustration below demonstrates the implementation of strength-based strategies and techniques.

Case Illustration

An 8-year old African-American boy, Deandere Williams and his 60 year -
old maternal grandmother, Mrs. Green, requested child and family outpatient
service due to Deandere having behavioral problems at school and problems with
overactivity at home. Deandere had two sisters living with him and his
grandmother. According to Mrs. Green his sister, Tanisha, 3, seemed to have
various developmental delays; and Deandere's sister Anita, 13, and had been
labeled autistic. Mrs. Green reported that she had hurt her leg approximately six
months ago and she now walks with a cane. At the intake session, Mrs. Green
vented frustration due to struggling to care for Deandere and his two sisters, who
have various special needs. Mrs. Green became tearful as she explained that she
spanked Deandere for the first time because she was trying to calm Anita during a
temper outburst and Deandere asked her the same question seven times. "I'm not
that kind of person, but I just get so frustrated when he demands all of my
attention at the hardest times." said Mrs. Green.

Upon talking with Deandere , the therapist found that Deandere had many
interests as he cheerfully reported that he loved animals and he wanted grandma to
take him to the zoo in the summer. He reported that he was interested in
computers and that he was going to get an "A" in Computers when he received his
next report card. Deandere was also curious. There were several times when he
asked questions: "Is there a doctor here ?"; "Will I get a shot ?"; "Do I have to
come to see you every day ?"; "How long will I get to see you ?"; and "Will
Grandma be with me all the time when I see you ?" Deandere was active during
the interview, he was able to keep busy with structured activities. He seemed to
enjoy drawing and he took pride in writing his own name. Mrs. Green seemed
proud of Deandere. She shared with therapist that Deandere "could be a very
good boy...but there are times when he gets on my last nerve with all of his
questions because he seems to ask many of his questions when I'm busy with the
other children". Mrs. Green went on to say that Deandere was the highest

21

functioning of the three children and he often helped her with the other children. She revealed that there were times when Deandere took on a lot if responsibility for his age and she felt guilty about that. "I guess that's why he asks so many questions. He needs to get some attention," she said.

The therapist noticed Deandere smile as Mrs. Green talked, and he asked if he could get Mrs. Green something to drink. Mrs. Green reminded Deandere that she had brought some crackers and juice which he could eat if he should get hungry. Toward the end of the interview, Deandere took the crackers and juice out of the bag, and was quiet and content.

When working with this family, the therapist noticed many obvious strengths. First, Mrs. Green demonstrated a great deal of love and concern for her grandson, Deandere. In addition, Deandere seemed to have a genuine love and concern for Mrs. Green. His protective attitude was demonstrated as he asked if he could get water for Mrs. Green; and the secure attachment was displayed by his hugs. Mrs. Green showed reciprocal feelings as she said many positive things about Deandere. Mrs. Green also showed the therapist that she was a survivor as she has been caring for three special needs children in less than adequate conditions. Despite her hurt leg and inadequate housing conditions, Mrs. Green had been able to attend to the needs of her children. As the therapist talked with Mrs. Green , she noticed that Mrs. Green was an excellent advocate for all three of her children. Mrs. Green's energetic positive attitude was demonstrated in various ways such as the volunteer work Mrs. Green did for the school in the morning; and her religious commitment and spirituality which was partly expressed by her church involvement. The church community seemed to be a significant source of support for Mrs. Green, and the social worker would be able to call on this source of religious commitment and spirituality at times when Mrs. Green and Deandere were feeling down.

The worker also recognized many strengths in Deandere. He had been able to achieve good academic grades, and he had extracurricular interests such as drawing and animals.

Creating a Service Plan

For social workers and therapists, the service plan is an important part of the counseling relationship. Service plans seem to be most helpful to the counseling process if the family works with the social worker to develop the plan. When working from a strength-based approach, the social worker may simply provide guidance while family members express what they would like to accomplish as a result of counseling. By taking this approach, social workers strengthen the relationship between the service provider and the client and a partnership begins to develop.

Once strengths had been identified and assessed, the social worker is in the position to develop a strength-based treatment plan. Based on the interview, the therapist, Mrs. Green, and Deandere identified the first goal as: **"Deandere will improve his citizenship grades a school by raising them from poor to average on three consecutive report cards".** Since Mrs. Green reported that Deandere had been having problems with hyperactivity at home, the second goal focused on this area: **"Deandere and grandma will report that Deandere's grandma rewards Deandere for good behavior at home at least four days per week for ten consecutive weeks".**

These goals focus on the increasing positive behavior rather than the decreasing of poor behavior. Here, the goal serves as the general statement regarding what the client wants to achieve in treatment. By using measurable goals workers will be able to work with the family to develop objectives that are also measurable.

While talking with Mrs. Green and Deandere, the therapist found that Deandere had monthly and weekly "star charts" which were used at school to reward his positive behavior. Therefore, it made sense for the worker to collaborate closely with the school, since the efforts of teachers and school staff could be quite helpful to Deandere and Mrs. Green as they work to improve

Deandere's behavior. This type of information contributed to the development of objectives which may be considered as "baby steps toward goals". Thus, upon examining the goal: **"Deandere will improve his citizenship grades at school by raising them from poor to average on three consecutive report cards,"** the therapist then talked with Deandere and Mrs. Green about things that she could help them with which would bring them closer to the achievement of their goals. Together they decided that Deandere could attend counseling every other week and he could bring both his weekly and monthly "star charts" to sessions. Mrs. Green reported to the worker that Deandere was currently receiving about two stars each week; she further stated that she and the teachers would like Deandere to improve this and they thought that with structure and support, Deandere could increase the number of stars he was receiving to four each week. Based on the information shared, the worker developed objectives listed under these goals as follows: "Deandere will bring weekly/monthly "star charts" to sessions and he will discuss any progress made regarding school behavior during nine consecutive months". The next objective was coordinated with this one: "Deandere will increase his number of good behavior stars from two to four per week for three consecutive weeks".

Next, the therapist examined the second goal with Deandere and his grandmother: **"Deandere and grandma will report that grandma rewards Deandere for good behavior at home at least four days per week for ten consecutive weeks."** Since this goal focused on Deandere's behavior at home, the therapist worked with Deandere and Mrs. Green to develop a list of reasonable rewards that Mrs. Green could give Deandere for good behavior at home. Upon the mention of rewards, the therapist noticed Mrs. Green's nervousness. Mrs. Green explained to the therapist that rewarding Deandere might be a good idea, but she expressed worry about having to buy the rewards on a limited income. The therapist agreed that giving material things as rewards could become expensive and seemed unrealistic. The therapist then explained that rewards for good behavior should be simple. These rewards could include having a favorite meal or being able to watch a favorite television show; staying up an hour later than usual; playing a favorite game; or verbal praise. Mrs. Green seemed to be comfortable with this type of reward system, and Deandere seemed excited. "I already do some of that, I guess I just never thought of it that way," reported Mrs. Green. After some discussion, the therapist, Deandere and Mrs. Green decided on two objectives which would serve as steps toward this second goal: **Objective a: "Deandere and grandma will develop a plan to reward good behavior at home and report using it 20 consecutive weeks;" and Objective b: "Deandere will find at least 5 positive ways to get grandma's attention."**

The second objective was formulated after Mrs. Green and the therapist discussed why Deandere might be acting out at home. Mrs. Green explained that much of her time is occupied in caring of her two other children who have various special needs. As this issue was further explored she and the therapist agreed that Deandere's acting out may simply be his way of saying "I love you and I want more of your attention." Thus, the therapist would focus on teaching Deandere to give Mrs. Green positive cues for attention and to ask for things that he needed.

Interventions

As one might guess, family therapy to focus on rewarding positive behaviors serves as one of the therapist's primary interventions in working with Deandere and Mrs. Green. The therapist also made plans to collaborate with school professionals in order to monitor Deandere's behavioral progress at school and to talk with teachers regarding what behavior management techniques might be successful with Deandere. Although the therapist worked from an outpatient program, she made plans to visit Deandere's home and school occasionally. The therapist felt that it was important to get to know Deandere's sisters and it was quite difficult for Mrs Green to transport these children to the agency. Thus occasional home visits would allow the therapist to see Deandere's home environment. These visits might be coordinated with those made by the case

25

manager. The referral for case management services made at intake would be helpful to assisting this family with gaining access to financial, household, and educational resources which had not yet been explored. Based on her recognition of the family strengths, the therapist was able to create a service plan which was consumer-driven rather than provider-driven. She felt confident that the family's chances of success were good. As the next four framework components are explored, strengths of specific relevance to low-income urban African-American families become more evident.

Knowledge Framework Component 2: Gender Roles

For many African-American families roles have evolved from a foundation based on African heritage. These roles have changed over the last two centuries as African-American families have sought to accommodate to mainstream America and cope with prejudice, racism and discrimination (McGoldrick, Pearce, & Giordano, 1982). Hines Boyd-Franklin (1982) point our that a major strength in African-American families may be found in the adaptability of family roles. Until recently, African-American families' strategies to cope with the stresses of racism were viewed as deviant because they differed from that of the dominant nuclear family norms of male and female role functions (McGoldrick, Pearce, Giordano, 1982). In order to help African-American families, it is critical to understand the roles played by family members and the relationships between family members.

Despite a history of stability in African-American families, male and female relationships today appear to be in a state of crisis which may be identified by what Elise B. Washington calls the "Uncivil War" (1996). Most African-Americans want a stable relationship which fulfills the basic human need to love and be loved, yet for a large number of African-Americans failed attempts to achieve such stability have resulted in emotional and spiritual strife leading to various tragic consequences such as child maltreatment; substance abuse; poor physical health; depression and even suicide in the African-American community. Observers of popular media can easily identify messages which indicate conflictual relationships between males and females in the Black community. Such messages emerge at Church conventions; in rap music lyrics; in the news; and in books and movies produced by African-Americans. In schools, homes, and on the job, African-Americans continue to express anger and frustration with the opposite sex

27

(Washington, 1996).

Considering the discord which occurs in many African-American male-female relationships, social workers may ask: "Where did it all start? and "How can I begin to understand the complex role dynamics which occurs between African-American males and females?" The most direct way to increase knowledge of male and female roles as well as gender conflict among African-Americans is to become familiar with the struggles and strengths which are specific to each gender.

Although all African-Americans face harsh societal challenges, African American men may face various unique struggles. What many refer to as the "endangerment of the African-American male (Gibbs, 1989)" is quite real. Issues which have particular significance for African-American men include unemployment; violence and trauma; health status; and crime and incarceration/imprisonment.

Unemployment represents a major problem for many African-American men. Some authors assert that one reason for the breakdown of the African-American family was the lack of employment opportunities for Black men (Washington, 1996). The closing of numerous plants in the United States has led to scarcity of high paying blue-collar jobs according to Washington (1996). The cause of such closures may have been the exportation of American jobs to cheaper overseas labor markets. David Driver (1992) offers statistics that are helpful in understanding economic factors related to the unemployment issues for African-American men. In the 1980's about 500,000 U.S. jobs were exported to Mexico's free trade zone where the prevailing wage was less than two dollars per hour (Driver, 1992). In the late 1980's 29% of America's foreign imports came from plants owned by American businesses. This maybe one variable among several which have contributed to the 32% unemployment rate among African-American men 20 to 44 years of age. Yet exportation of African-American jobs to cheap overseas labor markets alone does not explain high unemployment of Black men.

28

Other variables may be educational preparation for employment and accessibility to jobs. Another issue which relates specifically to the role of African-American men is violence. A 1988 Los Angeles study of homicides revealed that victims were primarily African-American and Hispanic males and between the ages of 15 and 24 years of age. In addition, the perpetrator of such crimes also fall within this age group(Barrett, 1991). Gibbs (1989) suggests the African-American male is an "endangered species" based upon the statistics cited above. There have been various explanations offered for violence among young African-American males. Although Wolfgang & Fetracuti's work is dated, it is still relevant. They attribute the overrepresentation of violent assault committed by African-American men to be linked to the ecological dynamics of inner city life and a subculture in which violence is perceived as a way of life (1967). This perspective may be identified as the "subculture of violence" thesis (Barrett, 1994). Critics of this thesis assert that this perspective does not give sufficient recognition to African-American history and the impact of slavery and racism on present-day crime. Exploration of this thesis should be done with consideration of critical viewpoints such as those of African-American scholars who stress the importance of seeing urban violence in the proper socioeconomical cultural context (Curtis, 1975; Rose & McClain, 1990). To expand upon this thesis, Curtis (1975) explains that there is a "multidimensional value space" model which addresses significant factors such as the interaction of race, culture, and violence present in urban settings. Although this thesis raises various points of interest, it is important to note that other factors such as socioeconomic, cultural, historical and political factors must be considered in order for one to begin a more complete exploration of the etiology of homicidal violence among African-American males.

The Psychoanalytic Thesis may be used in order to further understand sex roles among African-American males as this approach attributes the high incidence of violence to the lack of strong coping skills which are needed to effectively deal with the frustration, anger, and even rage which may come from situations such as

29

unemployment, poverty, discrimination or past traumas. If one is to consider a consumer's strengths, thinking from this perspective may seem to be a contradiction since part of this approach indicates a lack of strong coping skills. However, one may consider the African-American male's anger and rage as an appropriate reaction to the adverse conditions such as poverty and unemployment; yet the violent behavior such as committing a crime may be viewed a s a negative expression of anger and rage. Thus, the goal of a social worker would be to assist the African-American male consumer with more constructive ways to express his anger and rage. Therefore, the social worker could build upon the consumer's strengths of being able to survive adverse conditions as well as having appropriate feelings in response to these conditions. Another explanation offered for violent behavior among young African-American males is that criminal violent behavior may be modeled and learned quite easily during adolescence, a developmental stage in which youths struggle to achieve individuation and identity; while also exploring counter-cultural expressions. For many African American youth, this may mean conforming to the pressure of gangs and "posses", which seem to be related factor to violent behavior among urban youth (Barrett, 1988). Many young African-American males use drugs and alcohol as a means of coping with various adverse situations. More African-American males, age 15 to 30 are victims of alcohol related homicides than any other race-sex-age group (Gary, 1981). When considering the "endangered species" concept, it is important to note that alcoholic and drugs are associated with the three primary causes of death among African-American males (i.e. homicide, suicide and accidental deaths) since drugs and alcohol decrease inhibitions and increase feelings of frustration which may result in aggression (Barrett, 1994).

Another explanation for violent behavior among youth may be found in a growing body of evidence which suggests that these youth are products of various social systems which have failed them (Kessler, Burgess, & Douglass, 1998). This theory has relevance for mental health professionals serving African-American

30

males today. It is important for us to be aware of how these young men have been treated in their schools, neighborhoods, families, communities and social service agencies. Research by Busch and colleagues (1988) supports this belief with a study with a sample of 1,956 juvenile delinquents. Findings of this study indicate that youth who kill have certain characteristics such as criminally violent family members, gang membership, educational difficulty, and alcohol and drug abuse (Busch, et al, 1988). As social workers and mental health professionals, we will either fail or succeed in our role to provide positive mental health services. Our own ability to collaborate with other social systems in regard to providing a strong supportive environment for young African-American males influences this population's participation in and benefits gained from mental health services. Finally, an explanation for the violent behavior of young African-American males is also offered in a thesis which asserts that youth have been socialized to value the life and welfare of white people more than that of people of color. As a result, it is believed that there is an increased probability for the victimization of minority youth within their own cultural groups. This theory relates to "Black on Black" crime and offers explanation for the pattern of violence among African-Americans and other ethnic minorities (Kessler, et al., 1988).

Many young African American men may express their masculinity through "cool pose", a form of communication marked by certain language, posturing, and other carefully constructed performances which serve to present the male as proud, strong, and in control (Majors & Billson, 1992). "Cool pose" may be considered as a strength for African-American males as it often serves as a coping mechanism; to make them visible, and to empower them however, it also hides feelings of doubt, insecurity and vulnerability, anger and even rage (De La Cancela, 1994). Thus, it keeps these young men alienated from others and does not allow them to explore and express deep emotions. Historically, the form of "coolness" known as *ashe* was present in African-American tribes such as the Yorubas of Western Nigeria, 900 B.C. (Bascom, 1969). Often this masculine

31

attitude which relates to the gender role of the African-American male is expressed through rap music, various forms of dance, and graffiti art. Such expression may be viewed as a strength and a positive coping mechanism for many reasons. For many of these young males this artistic expression of music, art or dance literally paid of and provided income as they overcame poverty and the lack of formal education. In the eighties, break dancing not only provided a creative recreational outlet for many young African-American males, it gave many adolescent Black males the opportunity to hustle some change on urban street corners. In addition, onlookers such as movie producers, choreographers, and advertisers, recruited break dancers and graffiti artists to work in various settings, saving many of these African-American youth from life on the streets. In fact, breakdancing has been perceived as a means of preventing urban violence when it became a form of dance and positive competition between males (Majors, 1991).

Much of the research done in this area reflects the many challenges black men face. Often, it seems that black men feel that they lack the power to change the state of economic deprivation; and thus, these feelings of helplessness and isolation are likely to create negative behaviors. For example, an unemployed black man with limited marketable job skills, may commit a crime in the midst of his desperation; or he may turn to drugs as a means of escape (Staples, 1987, p. 10). As stated by Williams (1984), poverty, combined with racial injustice provides "fertile soil for criminal violence" (p. 289). In order to be helpful to black men struggling to overcome various challenges, social workers may find most success as they take on the role of activist (Allen-Meares & Burman, 1995). As activists, social workers offer hope to replace despair by helping black men to come up with concrete solutions to alleviate daily problems (Allen-Mearas & Burman, 1995). Thus, one might hope that each black man's individual striving supported by the activist role of the social worker may reduce "high risk status of African-American males in this society", (Gary & Leashore, 1982, p. 57).

Implications for Social Work Services

A challenge for social workers is to engage African-American adult males. The first step is to maintain and increase our historical knowledge of the African-American male role and how this relates to social services. It is important to understand the role of African-American fathers. One explanation for the decline in two parent African-American families is that Black men find themselves unable to provide for their basic needs of their families, and thus, some feel forced to leave their households so that their families may become eligible for government assistance and medical benefits (McGoldrick et al., 1991). Thus, although Black fathers have many strengths, their efforts are often undermined by external forces. Furthermore, it is important to recognize that the absence of a father from a household does not mean that all fathers/husbands lack contact with their wives or children. Even in cases where fathers/husbands do not maintain contact, it is typical for children to maintain contact with paternal extended family (McGoldrick et al., 1991).

Generally, the purpose of engagement is for the family and the worker to explore the nature of the relationship which leads to the development of a natural contract regarding the expectations of what future family work will involve (Raider, 1989). In beginning to explore the engagement process in family therapy with low-income, urban, African-American families, gaining each family member's trust becomes primary. This observation is supported in the author's research, in which 48% of the families workers stated that in "most" of the low-income, urban, African-American families whom they work, it was important to gain the trust of the family leader (s). Boyd-Franklin (1990) also supports this finding indicating that gaining trust is important to beginning the therapy process. If family workers are therapeutically creative, there are numerous options for gaining family trust, and thus, beginning the engagement process with the family. One way to begin to build a trusting relationship with a family is to demonstrate the worker's cultural awareness and willingness to learn from the families. The following case

33

illustration demonstrates the engagement of an African-American father and his family.

Case Illustration.

The Porter family, for example fulfills the profile of a family which could have been difficult to engage. Yet, the family worker's display of cultural awareness regarding African-American male and female roles combined with an evident willingness to involve extended family members helped her succeed in the successful engagement of the father, Mr. Porter.

The family was referred to the family preservation worker as a result of Mrs. Porter, a 32-year-old African-American mother calling a crisis line. Mrs. Porter stated that "things are starting to get out of control." She went on to explain to the crisis worker that Mr. Porter, 35, had recently returned home to live with her an their 15-year-old son, Leroy. At the time that Mrs. Porter called, Leroy and his father were yelling at each other. Leroy was attempting to leave the house to go to a party. Mr. Porter stated that it was 10:00 p.m., and that it was much too late for Leroy to be going to a party. In response, Leroy yelled, "You don't make the rules around here. You've been gone for a long time. Things are different now." At this point Leroy headed for the door. Mr. Porter physically grabbed him to stop him from leaving, and when Leroy resisted Mr. Porter struck him. Mrs. Porter feared that "things would get out of control" and called the police. The policeman was able to get Leroy to stay home for the night; while Mr. Porter agreed to spend the night at a neighbor's house "to cool off".

Once the referral was given, the family preservation worker called the Porters immediately, the next morning. She talked at length with Mrs. Porter who seemed overwhelmed and eager to share her dilemma. Mrs. Porter went on to say that Mr. Porter would be reluctant to speak with the worker. She stated that Mr. Porter was home now, but he was upset with her for "telling some stranger our

34

family business". After explaining the problem to Mrs. Porter, the worker asked to speak with Mr. Porter. Mr. Porter accepted, but was hesitant. Mr. Porter immediately asked if the worker was going to take his only boy away from him. The worker calmly explained that the purpose of family preservation was to keep families together and children at home. Mr. Porter was suspicious. The conversation continued as follows:

Mr. Porter: You know, I work during the day, so I don't have time to see you all day. And another thing, ... I really think I can handle my own family problems without the help of social workers.

Worker: We are not going to tell you what to do or how to handle your family. You're in charge. We can however, help you and Mrs. Porter to find your own solutions.

Mr. Porter: I just don't know.

Worker: My co-worker (The team approach was previously explained) and I are willing to come to your home after you get home from work. On evening visits, we often bring a dessert, something to share while we talk. Is it possible that you, Leroy and Mrs. Porter would be willing to spend an hour talking with us this evening.

Mr. Porter: I just don't want to be attacked. I made some mistakes. I had to leave my family for a while to my life together. Now at least I have a full-time job and I can stay with them. I'm trying to be a good father. Leroy doesn't appreciate me.

Worker: It must be discouraging when it seems like you work hard, and then attacked or your efforts are not appreciated.

Mr. Porter: You got it.

Worker: If you decide to meet with us, is there someone who could be at this meeting to give you a little support so that you don't feel attacked? A friend, a relative...?

Mr. Porter: Uh...Yeah (seems to be taken by surprise) Could my neighbor, Joe,

	be there? He's a good buddy. He knows my family inside out. I stayed at his house last night.
Worker:	That sounds like a great idea. Are you willing to try a meeting tonight to see if it might be helpful to you?
Mr. Porter:	I'll give it a try but if it isn't useful I don't want to be obligated to do it again.
Worker:	We can be there between 5:00 and 7:00 p.m. What time is good for you?
Mr. Porter:	Six o'clock is good for us. Is that OK? Oh, by the way, you said you'll bring a dessert, right?
Worker:	Certainly. What kind of dessert would you like?
Mr. Porter:	Well, all of us like donuts. Is that OK?
Worker:	Sure, so my co-worker and I will see you at 6 p.m. and we'll bring donuts--enough for six of us. You, Leroy, Mrs. Porter and your friend, Joe.

Due to the worker's cultural awareness of African-American male and female roles, she was able to understand some of the struggles faced by Mr. Porter. During the first meeting, the workers learned that Mr. Porter was separated from his family and that he spent time in two foster homes. He shared his worry that this might happen to Leroy. The workers assured him that they would work to keep his family together, and Joe gave Mr. Porter support as he stated that he had participated in a similar family preservation program, and that his child remained at home. It was evident that the workers' willingness to include Joe in the meeting played a key role in engaging Mr. Porter. Here, the worker's concern not to undermine Mr. Porter's autonomy as well as awareness of the value of extended family for African-Americans was essential. The workers' flexibility was also key to engaging the family. The willingness to forget traditional business hours played a critical role in the engagement process.

To help families to trust them, family workers may also use the simple technique of addressing the families' concrete needs. Many practice models which focus on strengthening high-risk families assert that addressing the family's immediate concrete needs should be the worker's first priority (Barthel, 1992a, 1992b; Chilman, 1966; Geismer & Krisber, 19967; Halper & Jones, 1981; Kaplan, 1986; McKinney, 1970; Rabin, Sens & Rosenbau, 1982; Wasik, Bryant & Lyons, 1990). Research involving low-income, urban, African-American families report that the families perceived concrete services as the most useful service that they received. Assisting families with concrete needs is paramount in the change process while presenting a mechanism to develop partnerships within a trusting relationship (Barthel, 1992a, 1992b; Fraser & Haapala, 1987-88; Morton & Brisby, 1993). For low-income families, assistance with concrete needs serves as a non-threatening, rapport-building intervention which may be helpful before delving further into the therapeutic process to explore psychological issues (Kaplan & Girard, 1994). Furthermore, assisting families so that concrete needs are met facilitates trust in the worker since family members come to believe that the worker is truly there to help them (Kaplan & Girard, 1994).

Early studies (Minuchin, Montalvo, Guerney, Rossman and Schumer, 1967) maintained that discord between African-American males and females tended to be dealt with in an indirect manner rather than through confrontation. Often, African-American women who may be more actively religious than their partners are labeled as "all-sacrificing" or the "strength of the family" (Hines & Boyd-Franklin, 1982, p. 89). These women often take on family responsibilities less frequently assumed by Caucasian women, and thus from a white middle-class perspective, their roles may be interpreted as dominant when they are not (Hines & Boyd-Franklin, 1982). Within the African-American community, male-female relationships have themselves, become skewed by economic factors and sex ratios (McGoldrick, et al., 1991). The unequal sex ratio is not new, since African-American women have outnumbered African-American men for nearly 150 years although the ratio has grown worse through the years (Staples, 1989). Various factors have contributed to this imbalance such as infant mortality, substance abuse rates, death related to hazardous jobs, delays in seeking health care, incarceration, military service and homicide (United States Bureau of the Census, 1989).

African-American female-headed households have also dramatically increased, from 25% in 1965 to 56% in 1990 (Baca Zinn & Eitzen, 1993). An important reason for this growth may be the increase in births to unmarried African-American women, which in 1990 was reported to be 57% (Pear, 1991). Some African-American women tend to place a higher value on the maternal role rather than the marital role (McGoldrick et al., 1989), and many middle and low-income African-American women are choosing to have children outside of marriage rather than to remain childless (Staples, 1985; Tucker & Mitchell-Kernan, 1991).

The shortage of marriageable male mates for African-American women may contribute to what has been identified as a major problem among African-American families, namely "children who must grow up without the resources and love that are found with more than one parent..." (McAdoo, 1995, p. 25). In 1989, 80% of African-American children had spent part of their life in a single-parent/caregiver home by the age of 17 years, in contrast with 46% with Caucasian children (Hernandez, 1993). According to the Census Bureau statistics (Ellwood and Crane, 1990), marriage among African-Americans has decreased from 64% in 1970 to only 44% of African-American adults married in 1991.

This rate reflects delayed marriage as well as high levels of divorce among African-Americans (Marital Status, 1991). The divorce rate for African-American women is twice that of other women. Although 80% of these women marry, many experience difficulty in staying married (McAdoo, 1995). McAdoo (1995) asserts that greater attention needs to be paid to single African-American mothers whose pregnancies begin after their teen years. Although single-parenting may present a problem for some African-Americans, it should be noted that "female-dominated" households were considered universal among poor African-American families even

38

when statistics showed otherwise (Leigh & Green, 1982). According to Leigh and Green, much of the literature which explores the "female-headed" model assumes from the outset of that this pattern is negative. Part of the problem with this type of research stems from its starting point: the idea that a household is the same thing as an independent nuclear family. A household and a family do not need to be recognized as identical social entities; the perception that the African American nuclear family is "disorganized" or "broken" illustrates this particular confusion which may be eliminated by examining the network that binds households together (Leigh & Green, 1982).

Many strengths may be seen in African-American women who have always played active roles in their families and communities. Jobs have been more available to them than to their male counterparts, and as a result, the economic survival of African-American families has often depended on women (McGoldrick et al., 1989). Pinderhuges (1982) recognized the role of the African-American mother as an example of flexibility and role compensation in the family. Further, she suggests that when the mothers function as the "strength" in a family, there are adaptive as well as maladaptive ramifications. The African-American mother's strength has been necessary to counteract the lack of cultural guidelines for family roles and the undermining of the male's father/husband role (Pinderhughes, 1982), which may be due to various discriminatory practices that limit the African-American male's opportunities to provide for his family as he would like (Hines & Boyd-Franklin, 1982).

When providing family therapy services, workers must demonstrate awareness of the effective coping strategies and strengths of African-American families (Daly, Jennings, Beckett & Leashore, 1995) as well as the many types of racism and racist system to which they have been exposed (Pinderhughes, 1982). In extreme instances of racism, the male has been so undermined in his role that he may become negative, irresponsible, exploitative, violent, remote or absent. If the mother cannot assume a strong role in situations such as these, the family will face serious trouble. Thus, the families' response to the stresses of racism will serve to either dissolve or reinforce family problems (Pinderhughes, 1982).

Knowledge Framework Component 3: The Extended Family

Understanding the historical development of the African American extended family and its importance to the African American helping tradition is critical for social workers today. Knowledge about the historical evolution of the African American extended family will make current trends more clear, thus increasing the cultural awareness of social workers. Exploration of this component will highlight changes which are specific to changes in the extended family for African-Americans living in urban areas.

Historically, the extended family has been viewed as a healing force in African American families (Littlejohn-Blake & Anderson-Darling, 1993). Despite diversity among African societies, most of them placed strong emphasis on kinship bonds. Small families often became part of larger family units. These larger family networks might become a clan; and many clans would form an entire tribe or community (Martin & Martin, 1985). African-American slave families were comprised of both biological and non-biological members. These non-biological family members were referred to as fictive kin. Enlarged families developed out of the need for survival as well as social obligation. Members of these families provided various forms of support such as helping new slaves with adjustment to a new plantation; caring for the ill; sharing resources; for worship and recreation; and planning escapes. In addition, it was important for the families to work together to establish a particular code of conduct since one slave's behavior could jeopardize the welfare of all slaves.

Two examples of mutual aid and fictive kinship during times of slavery were the care of older slaves and child-rearing practices in these communities. Since elderly slaves could not work as has as younger slaves, this lowered their worth in the eyes of their masters. Therefore, younger slaves would often help older slaves to do their work or meet quotas (Owens, 1976). Often old slaves who

41

were ill and difficult to care for were set free or sold cheaply (Owens, 1976 p.49). Many older slaves seemed to use strong kinship bonds as a coping mechanism to deal with the difficulties of their lives. Consistent with past African tradition, members of the community treated the aged with a great deal of respect, and the aged held places of honor in their families. Often the aged were perceived to be the head of the family. They filled many important roles such as child-rearing, and teaching African-American children what was essential for survival (Martin & Martin, 1985).

Although child-rearing represented a primary concern among parents who were slaves parents who worked on plantations often had little time to look after their children. Children whose parents died, became ill, or were sold to other plantations, were cared for by relatives or fictive kin as they were naturally transitioned into existing households. The task of socializing children into the roles of slavery fell to the older slaves in the community. According to historical accounts, children were treated on the basis of equality; and thus, they were barely aware of their status as slaves (Blassingame, 1972). Therefore, when these youngsters reached the age when serious work was expected of them, older slaves and other care givers were forced to make children learn their duties as slaves. This socialization process involved teaching children to relinquish behaviors which might be considered rebellious, aggressive or insubordinate in the eyes of the slave masters since such behavior might get the children, their parents and other community members into serious trouble (Martin & Martin, 1985). Children were taught not to verbally confront slave masters and they were also taught to keep silent about family affairs. Aged slaves taught the older children to help with caring for the young children. Important values which were promoted among children of this African-American heritage was those of mutual support; and a sense of obligation to the welfare of those in the extended family as well as those in the slave community.

Children were taught traditional African values both verbally and by

42

example.   The strengths of these African American communities were clearly reflected in the way that family members cared for the aged and the ill and shared their limited resources. The sharing of resources and mutual aid extended across different status groups which existed among Black slaves. Although slavery did not allow the emergence of social classes, it did permit the formation of status groups. On the plantations, three broad status groups formed: house slaves; field slaves; and skilled slaves. In order to survive, these three groups cooperated and provided mutual support to one another. The spirit of closeness which developed between the three groups was largely due to the existence of the extended family in the slave community (Martin & Martin, 1985). Many slaves had family members who belonged to different status groups; and they found it difficult to look down upon their family. Thus, loyalty to extended family helped to promote hospitality between the three status groups. In addition, it was common for some slaves to work in both homes and fields, maintaining status in both groups (Genovese, 1974).

The sense of closeness between the three groups was demonstrated by various means of mutual support. House slaves were better off economically better off than field slaves, so they were able to provide field slaves with food, clothing, tobacco, and other needed and desired items. In addition, house slaves provided information to field slaves which helped field slaves to plan escapes or simply to survive (Owens, 1976). There was also mutual support between skilled slaves and field slaves. Skilled slaves were also given higher status than field slaves, and their image was one of pride and independence (Genovese, 1974, p. 392 & 393). Often, skilled slaves taught field slaves their trades and secretly taught them and other slaves to read and write. Skilled slaves provided means of communication as they traveled from town to town. Such travel brought them in contact with other slaves and free African-Americans. Thus, skilled Blacks became valuable sources of news and vital information.

Although extended family and fictive kin had equal significance in the lives

43

of free Blacks, their exposure to larger world facilitated a different view of racial consciousness than that held by slaves. For free Blacks, kin consciousness meant racial consciousness since this group developed an awareness of the common struggles of African Americans. They believed that progress and advancement for African American people were more likely to occur due to group rather than individual efforts. These free African-Americans became known to many as the first generation of race conscious Blacks. Therefore, these free Blacks become known as "race men" and "race women" (Drake & Cayton, 1945). The major concern of these African-Americans was the survival and liberation of the Black community. As they worked toward the welfare of all Black people, this group's efforts were demonstrated in various ways. These men and women defended their race against mainstream propaganda which portrayed Blacks as an inferior race. They acted as motivational speakers and encouraged African-Americans to learn to read and write so that they could gain knowledge about their heritage. Race men and women promoted the message that educated Blacks who carried themselves in manner respectful of African-American traditions were a credit to the Black race, while those who were disrespectful of African-American traditional values were blight on the race and were accused of bringing down the entire Black race To promote racial pride, these men and women, believed that it was important to educate young Blacks about their African-American heritage.

The racial consciousness among the free Blacks prompted the institutionalization of the Black mutual aid system. This helping system differed from those which existed among slaves. Slaves tended to use fewer formal support systems; while free African-Americans formally organized mutual aid efforts through the building of institutions such as churches, schools and fraternal orders (Martin & Martin, 1985).

Consistent with African-Americans support systems under slavery, the primary support system among free Blacks was the extended family. The extended family continued to function as the dominant force in the African-American helping

44

tradition after the Civil War and during the Reconstruction. The Reconstruction was a time when Black people were met with the challenges of trying to rebuild lives which were degraded by slavery and to educate former slaves so that they could move from slavery to citizenship (Martin & Martin, 1985). One major struggle was that of poverty. Many Black families needed food, clothing, shelter, and medical care. Due to oppression and racism, many African-Americans felt as if they were outsiders. They needed to become independent from white masters and to begin to recognize their capacity as talented independent individuals. Based on these needs, extended family, women's groups, the Black churches, and other institutions worked together to help African-Americans to rebuild their lives. However, efforts made during the Reconstruction were not always met with success. The mainstream population had not yet accepted the freedom of the Black people. This was evidenced by terrorism by groups such as the Klu Klux Klan; lynchings; and incidents of Black voter harassment (Martin & Martin, 1985). Although many Reconstruction efforts were met with disappointment, such efforts demonstrated the helping tradition which, in many ways, would be passed on to future generations.

The African-American helping tradition remained prevalent in both urban and rural cultures. Black racial consciousness facilitated the development of organizations which worked to improve the lives of African-Americans: The Nation Association for the Advancement of Colored People; the Universal Negro Improvement Association; and the National Urban League (Martin & Martin, 1985).

Changes occurred in the ways that mutual support manifested itself. During the early part of the twentieth century, new efforts geared toward Black advancement included homes for girls; and recreational centers and parks which provided safe places for children (Martin & Martin, 1985). Although these represented a more formal means of helping than past traditions, they could be perceived as being a further evolution of the African-American extended family.

It is clear the Black helping tradition continues to exist today. However, helping mechanisms today may be quite different from those which originated in Africa. It is important to consider the migration to urban area, the pressures by dominant mainstream society, and racism.

As many African-Americans sought a better life in the city, the extended family played a significant role. Many Blacks were motivated to migrate to cities because extended family members were living there. Often these extended family members provided a place to stay until these loved ones could find housing of their own (Martin & Martin, 1985). Reactions to city life have been the focus of various studies and may provide insight into current trends which social workers see today. Fraizer (1969) proposed that after an individual had lived in the city for a while, he/she began to shed ways related to traditional/rural life. However, Martin & Martin (1985) suggest that some previously rural African-Americans resisted the influences of urban life. In order to do this, many African-Americans "carved" a small town out of a large city in order to make city life less overwhelming. These individuals associated primarily with extended family or fictive kin in the same city. Again, the extended family was used as a means of coping. In this case, the extended family gave those in the city a sense of personal connection in the impersonal city.

Despite their migration to the cities, most small-town African-Americans had ties to their rural origins. Although they may have lived in the cities for 20 or 30 years, they were likely to consider their small-town origin as "home" (Grier & Cobbs, 1968). Rural African-American migrants who tried to maintain small-town attitudes and behaviors were forced to fit in with the ways of city life. Their friends and relatives were likely to warn them that city people were not to be trusted. It was explained to them that practices such as greeting people; leaving cars and homes unlocked and stopping to help someone would only lead to trouble in the city (Martin & Martin, 1985). Black migrants from rural areas were often criticized by city-bred Blacks for exhibiting small-town behaviors. Thus, the

46

communal spirit and helping traditions which were traditionally present among African-Americans began to fade. To some extent, the growth of the urban population changed the spirit of helping traditions among African-Americans. Unlike the times of slavery and the Reconstruction, these Blacks were living in an environment in which helping others was not considered conducive to survival.

However, despite the changes and the perceived decline in Black helping traditions, the extended family continues to be essential to Black survival (Martin & Martin, 1985); and kinship bonds among African-Americans remain strong today (Littlejohn-Blake & Anderson-Darling, 1993). It is especially important for Black families living in urban areas as it is one of the few care-giving institutions which has remained available to them. Although the role of the extended family played a much larger role in the past, the extended family was still responsible for providing jobs to many urban African-Americans and for providing support to the elderly. Three African-American extended family helping traditions which continue to be important today include the practice of informal adoptions; care of the elderly; and the helping role of grandparents. Another important helping tradition previously demonstrated by extended family involves care for children with developmental or congenital disabilities. Often, helping practices provided by the extended family becomes apparent when services are unavailable or inaccessible (especially to poor, urban families), and family networks become quite salient in their response (Daly, Beckett, Jennings, & Leashore, 1995). For African-Americans, the family relationship becomes even more important when a family member is unable to obtain assistance from mainstream institutions (McGoldrick, et. al. 1991). An example is that of African-American parents of children born with developmental or congenial disabilities. Generally, these children were well cared for at home and were integrated into the community. Many parents made this decision, in part because there were few residential facilities available to African-Americans. Families without many financial resources tended to rely on informal support systems (Daly, Jennings, Beckett, &

Leashore, 1995). Since use of these networks has been creative and positive in the Black community, social workers must view such extended family practices as strengths.

The diversity and adaptability of family roles (Hill, 1971) may be illustrated by the example of informal adoption among African-American families (Boyd-Franklin, 1990). Informal adoption takes place when children of relatives, friends or extended family are adopted on the basis of informal understandings between the biological parent and the adoptive parent. This arrangement bypasses the legal system and the courts. In most of these situations, biological parents desire to keep their children; yet they are aware that they may not be able to provide adequately for their children at the time when the informal adoption occurs. Many biological parents have plans to provide adequate homes and to be reunited with their children as soon as possible after the informal adoption takes place. In the interim they feel more confident and comfortable knowing that their children are being cared for by family or extended family and they hope to be able to care for their children some time in the future (Franklin, 1989). For the most part, the process of informal adoption is regarded neither as neglect nor as a rejection, and the length of these arrangements is not always predetermined. Arrangements planned as temporary may become permanent due to the emotional bonds which develop during care-giving (McGoldrick, et. at. 1991).

Based on this author's experience, social workers who serve low-income urban African-American families may encounter agency problems related to informal adoption. Social services agencies require that a legal guardian or biological parent give consent for a child to receive services. Therefore, if the child is in need of services and has an informal primary caregiver such as a grandmother, the grandmother would not be able to give or send for the child to receive services due to the lack of legal documentation of her guardianship. Although informal adoption is a strength which has been a part of the African-American helping tradition (Daly, Beckett, Leashore & Jennings, 1995), it may create obstacles to the provision of social services. The dilemma for the social worker is to maintain a balance between respect for African-American helping traditions and complying with legal requirements which exist within the social service organization.

Care for the elderly represents an example of how the extended family contributes to the African-American helping tradition. Although a variety of managers exist to care for the elderly among low income African-Americans, it is most often extended family members who care for them (Thornton, 1995). In some cases, the availability of Medicare and Medicaid has led to increased use of health-related and social services (Davis et. al., 1989); however, the poor and minority populations often have difficulty paying medical expense since they cannot afford private medical health insurance supplements. Over the past decade, access to formal services has been further restricted due to the government's attempt to reduce its share of hospital and nursing home costs. Thus, informal providers within the extended family have often assumed the responsibility of caring for African-American elderly individuals (Thornton, 1995).

As previously discussed kinship networks in African-American families have flexibility rather than being rigidly defined (McGoldrick, et. al., 1991) and there is a great deal of respect given to African-American grandparents. Most of the literature on the grandparents' role is focused on the African American grandmother. As early as 1939, Frazier named African-American grandmothers as the guardians of generations. For many African-American women, motherhood and grandmotherhood represent important social roles. The socialization process to prepare women for these important roles begins during childhood, providing for social role identity (Hoffman & Wyatt, 1960; Jackson, 1971, Martin & Martin, 1978). Regardless of whether they live in the family household or independently, most African-American grandmothers are looked upon as part of the nuclear family and play active roles in the lives of family members (Burton & Bengston, 1985; Comer, 1980, Hill, Foote, Aldous, Carlson, & MacDonald, 1978; Jackson,

1971; Stack, 1974; Yelder, 1976).

This assertion is supported by the findings of a survey conducted by Timberlake and Chipungu (1992). Their study was conducted with 200 middle-class grandmothers of elementary-school-aged children living in urban communities. According to findings in this study, more than four out of five of the grandmother respondents reported that they perceived their grandchildren as an expansion of self, to continue beyond their own lives, as a means of keeping family traditions. Eighty-one percent of those participating scored the moral or altruistic aspects of grandparenting as significant; 75% of the participants rated the dimension of power as important. For these grandmothers, the terms power and influence were defined as opportunities for providing guidance; teaching; and impacting future generations in addition to the control over material and emotional resources. (Timberlake & Chipungu, 1992 p. 209).

Furthermore, findings of the authors' own research, which focused on social services to low-income urban African American families, support assertions in this section to the effect that the extended family fulfills an important role among low-income, urban African Americans. Respondents in the authors' study were social workers, case-managers and therapists who provided services to low-income, urban, African American families. On a Likert scale, 40% of these respondents reported that "many" or "most" of the families whom they served received help from extended families. Respondents also reported that 80% of these families regarded their extended family as important. The role of grandparents was also explored and 48% of the professionals surveyed reported that grandparents served as primary care givers in "many" or "most" of their cases. Furthermore, participants indicated that these African American grandparents play strong roles in their families in "many" or "most" of the families with whom they work.

Informal adoption, care for the elderly, and the role of the African American grandparents are only three examples of how the African-American helping tradition is demonstrated through the extended family. Despite many political, economic, and social barriers which have often interfered with African-American family life, the extended family clearly remains a strength among today's African-Americans (Timberlake & Chipungu, 1992). Literature on the extended family household indicates that there are various economic benefits which come from these arrangements, and the extended family often serves as a means of pooling limited resources (Thornton, 1995). Emotional support has also been recognized as a resource provided as a result of close extended family ties in the Black community (Taylor, et. al. 1990). When considering family strengths, it should also be noted that many Black families have been able to remain attached to their extended families in a manner comparable to that of immediate families (Thornton, 1995). For social workers, it is important that extended family relationships such as this not be assessed using conventional/traditional models of family and community life. On a larger scale, it is also important for policy-makers to discard these traditional models during the process of policy development since Afro-centric traditions, such as devotion to elders, is less valued in such frameworks (Thornton, 1995).

In summary, the extended family in the Black community proves unique in its ability to willingly absorb distant or non-biological members into its households and kinship networks (Fine, Schebel, & James Meyers, 1987). Close relationships with individual members provide economic and moral support which assists families in daily living and in times of crises (Littlejohn-Blake & Anderson-Darling, 1993). In addition, the pooling of limited resources, is also related to the presence of the extended family. The inclusion of extended family members in these households is associated with the flexibility of financial provider and domestic roles (Thornton, 1995). When working with low-income, urban, African-American families, social workers may wish to learn more about the presence of the extended families in the lives of the consumers whom they serve. It may be helpful to welcome and include extended family members in therapy sessions and other

51

meetings. The following case illustration demonstrates how knowledge of the African-American extended family component can be applied to social work practice.

Case Illustration

The identified client, Tony Smith, is an 11 year-old African-American boy who came to a community mental health center in a child and family program. He visited the center after he was hospitalized for sexually acting out and threatening girls in his class with sexual harm. Tony came to his first family session after being hospitalized with his 35 year-old Uncle Bob. Uncle Bob explained that he and his mother, Ms. Smith (Tony's maternal grandma), have been Tony's primary care givers since Tony was 8 years-old, right after the death of Tony's mother. Uncle Bob reported that Tony never knew his father and that his whereabouts were unknown at this time. Although the threats were not as severe, Uncle Bob reported that Tony was still making inappropriate comments to girls in his class. Uncle Bob expressed concern because Tony often looked sad and seemed to daydream a lot. Uncle Bob explained that Tony's teacher, Ms. W., also noticed the same sad expressions and daydreaming at school, and Ms. W. told Uncle Bob that Tony was failing two classes because he was not handing in his work. Tony denied that he had been sexually abused at first, but two sessions later, he admitted that a male friend of his mother's molested him while his mother was out of the house.

During the initial interview, the therapist, 35 year-old, Mr. Mac, made sure to ask questions which would be helpful to providing services which fit well with the family's needs. First, he sought to gather information in order to identify major goals. The goals identified were: 1) Tony will have positive interactions with female peers and he will refrain from sexually acting out; and 2) Tony will use positive coping skills to work through trauma, grief and loss issues which limit his performance at school and at home.

By asking the right questions initially, Mr. Mac gathered information which he could use to help Tony meet his goals. During this first session, Tony and his Uncle Bob were present:

Mr. Mac: Who lives at home with you and Tony?

Uncle Bob: Well, there is his Grandma Smith who helps take care of him, and his cousins, Sam, who is 13; and Ed who is 11.

Mr. Mac: How do you get along with everyone at home, Tony?

Tony: I get along with Ed and Sam really good, but Grandma gets mad at me a lot because I don't do chores when she wants me to. (Looking over at Uncle Bob.) I guess he's mad at me now too because of what happened at school.

Uncle Bob: Yes, I was upset, but now we're here to get help. Grandma and I care about you. We just can't have you acting this way. We get frustrated and tried. I'm tired of working so hard and then having to run to school for you so often. We have to do something to solve these problems you're having.

Mr. Mac: Your uncle is very concerned about you, Tony.

Uncle Bob: That's right. He calls me Uncle Bob, but I love him like I love Sam and Ed. I love him like I love my own sons.

Later in the interview:

Mr. Mac: What do you like to do, Tony?

Tony: Well, I like playing basketball with Sam and Ed. I like to go to Church on Sunday, and seeing Pastor Tom. I like to go to the arcade with him (Uncle Bob), and I like to draw.

Mr. Mac: Is there anything that you enjoy doing with your Grandma?

Tony: Like I was saying before, she and I don't always get along; but when she's not mad at me I do like to listen to her stories.

Mr. Mac: What are the stories about?

Tony: They're about Uncle Bob when he was little and about Pastor Tom when she first met him. Sometimes she talks about my Mom and I get a little sad.

Uncle Bob: See, Tony loves Grandma, but he just doesn't like all of her rules. A lot of the time she provides the discipline; and then because she's 75 she asks Tony to help her with a lot of things and sometimes it seems to her like he's lazy, but I guess he's just daydreaming most of the time.

Based on his initial interview, Mr. Mac recognized Grandma Smith's care giver role in the family. It was also evident that Tony and Uncle Bob have a great deal of respect for Grandma Smith. Mr. Mac began to identify several family strengths during the initial interview. Strong family bonds and loyalty were evidenced by Uncle Bob and Grandma Smith's taking care of Tony. Although only Uncle Bob was documented as Tony's legal guardian, Grandma Smith was an informal care-giver, and had a great deal of power in the family. Since Grandma Smith played an important role in the family, Mr. Mac worked to engage her in family sessions. Mr. Mac also made a note to use Uncle Bob, Ed, and Sam as positive role models since Tony seemed to get along well with them. Another strength was noted in the family's bond with Pastor Tom. Since Tony reported that Grandma Smith told stories about when she first met Pastor Tom, Mr. Mac further explored the family's relationship to Pastor Tom. Uncle Bob and Tony explained that Pastor Tom had known Grandma Smith for more than 20 years; and Pastor Tom was considered part of the family.

As Mr. Mac wrote his service plan, he referred to the initial information gathered, and continued to talk with Tony and Uncle Bob about ways that Tony might reach the two goals identified. Tony's first goal involved having positive interactions with female peers without sexually acting out. Mr. Mac identified Uncle Bob, Ed, Sam and Pastor Tom as positive male role models in Tony's life. Thus, he asked Uncle Bob if he, Sam, Ed and Pastor Tom would be willing to participate in role-modeling exercises in which they would assist with modeling positive interactions with female peers. Both Tony and Uncle Bob were excited

54

about the idea of including Pastor Tom in their sessions. Tony asked if he could have some sessions with only Pastor Tom and Mr. Mac present since there were things that he was afraid to share with the rest of his family members at this time. Since Pastor Tom was considered to be a part of the family, Uncle Bob said that he was comfortable with Tony doing this. Uncle Bob further stated that he thought Pastor Tom could help him to understand that some of Tony's behaviors were often upsetting to him and the other family members. Mr. Mac noted that Pastor Tom's support might also be used as a means of helping Tony to develop effective coping skills to deal with the grief and loss in his life. Mr. Mac began with a session with Pastor Tom in order to help Tony to identify the sources of his sexually acting out and the explore other ways that Tony might cope rather than sexually acting out. Since Grandma Smith felt especially uncomfortable with Tony's sexually acting out, Mr. Mac then set up a session with Grandma Smith, Pastor Tom and Tony in which Pastor Tom played the role of co-therapist and explained to Grandma Smith reasons why Tony sexually acted out and what she could do to help. Grandma Smith seemed comfortable asking Pastor Tom questions and she seemed relieved to hear from Pastor Tom that Tony was not a "bad kid" and that she was doing a good job taking care of him. Once the family's discomfort with Tony's sexually acting out behaviors was reduced, Tony became more at ease with talking to Uncle Bob, Pastor Tom, and Grandma Smith about past trauma, grief and loss, and Mr. Mac worked with the family to support Tony in his use of positive coping skills (his second goal). During one session, Tony and Mr. Mac brainstormed a list of coping skills which Tony might use. Tony then narrowed the list down and chose coping skills which were most likely to work for him. During a family session, Tony informed family members of the coping skills he was going to use and he let each family member know how he/she might be of help. To begin, Tony identified the coping skills of talking to Pastor Tom, other family members and Mr. Mac; and keeping a journal. Tony acknowledged that he could be forgetful and he asked Grandma Smith to help him with keeping up with his journal writing. Since Grandma Smith provided much of the discipline in the home, she did a good job making a rule that 4-4:30 p.m. was journal writing time for Tony, and the plan was for this to become part of Tony's routine.

For Tony and his family, the extended family represented a source of strength and support. Thus, it was clinically appropriate to use this strength to help Tony achieve his service plan goals. Objectives and interventions therefore focused on the involvement and support which came from Tony's extended family and they played an active role in helping Tony to succeed. For this family, there also seemed to be a strong sense of spirituality which supported the family bonds. Pastor Tom played an important role not only as part of the extended family, but as a means of expression of the family's spirituality and a means of spiritual support. For this family and for many other low-income, urban, African-American families spirituality represents a strength as well as a coping skill. Thus, the component of spirituality will be further explored in the next section of this framework.

Knowledge Framework Component Four: Religion, The Black Church and Spirituality

It is important to identify the difference between spirituality, religion, and the church. Universally, people, including social service professionals, use the terms religion and spirituality interchangeably, and thus, incorrectly (Beverly, 1995). Religion may be defined as an organized set of attitudes, beliefs, and practices which vary according to one's denomination. Often, religion contains a great deal of dogma and doctrine (Beverly, 1995).

Spirituality, on the other hand, does not require denominational affiliation, and it is not limited by doctrine. Although spirituality is universal, meaning that it may be applied to all individuals at some level, it is also particular to each individual (Beverly, 1995). Therefore, one can be spiritual without professing a belief in a particular religion; yet one can also be religious as well as spiritual (Beverly, 1995). The church may be defined as a congregation of people who have come together to express and uphold a particular set of religious beliefs. The church bears similarity to religion since both of these terms are much more concrete and may be explained more easily than spirituality. The church differs from religion since it represents the congregation of people rather than a particular belief system.

The Black Church

To understand the importance of the Church to African-American families, one must first have some knowledge of its history. At the turn of the century, many African-Americans experienced a prevailing spirit of creativity and optimism. This spirit was vigorously motivated by the African-American Church (Bagley & Carroll, 1995). African-American survived numerous tragedies, such as the bewilderment of emancipation from slavery, reconstruction of the South, and the pathos of depression. Therefore, a majority of African-Americans have suffered

57

from a "post-oppressive reaction syndrome." Post-oppressive reaction syndrome may be defined as the psychological effects as a result of the experiences previously mentioned (Anderson, 1988; Hines & Boyd-Franklin, 1982; Billingsley, 1968). In response to society's many oppressive forces, various manifestations occurred. These include rage, self-debilitating behaviors, somatic pathology, antisocial acting-out, crime, depression, isolation and weakened social interactions (Hines & Boyd-Franklin, 1982; Billingsley, 1968).

Despite the numerous struggles African-American families have encountered, their religious institutions have served as a support (Hill, 1978; Bagley & Carroll, 1991). As African-Americans have moved beyond various debilitating effects, such as post-oppressive reaction syndrome, a major healing force was found in the Church (Poole, 1990). In order to mobilize resources denominations of the African-American Church dropped their denominational separation. As a result, they built a coalition of strength, courage, and progress. The coalition consisted of Black Methodist, Baptist, Holiness, Presbyterian, Pentecostal, and Muslim congregations which briefly existed as the Black Church.

Historically, the African-American Church served its people by providing them with ways to renew their spirit, inspire and restore hope, gain peace and relief, and promote growth. For example, the African-American Church played an integral role in the formation of the underground railroad. Up until the emancipation, the African-American Church served as a source of education as it provided a meeting place and an outlet for oratory, physical, and cultural arts such as industry, singing, music, dancing and prose. In addition, the Church offered organizational, administrative, and leadership opportunities for people restricted from free expression (Bagley & Carroll, 1995). After the emancipation, however, only inadequate textbooks in segregated schools were offered. Prior to the emancipation, the church acted as an unparalleled leadership training forum (Bagley & Carroll, 1995.) Many African-Americans aspired to the ministry, the only "acceptable" form of leadership (Woodson, 1972).

The African-American Church has reached out to serve all of the community's functions in all social classes, often within the same structure (McAdoo & Crawford, 1991). Here, the African-American Church played many roles. Through industrialization, the African-American Church remained paramount. This was an era during which the Caucasian community resisted serving African-Americans, so the Church created useful alternatives. The Church often acted as the welfare department; an insurance provider, hospice and respite for the sick and those in need (McAdoo & Crawford, 1991). The Church also inspired the spirit of achievement, an essential part of spirituality within many African-Americans. African-American Churches gave birth to various opportunities such as job-matching services, housing corporations, banks, business ventures, schools, universities, and other service agencies (Bagley & Carroll, 1995). When African-Americans were discriminated against and denied access to education, the Church community created its own institutions of learning such as Arkansas Baptist College (Beverly, 1995). In response to Caucasian banks' refusal to lend money to African-American entrepreneurs and prospective homeowners, the Church created its own credit union (Bagley & Carroll, 1995). To facilitate growth, Mount Olivet Baptist Church in New York laid the ground work for the YWCA, providing affordable housing to young women coming into the city to work. In response to African Americans' limited access to health care, churches such as Saint Stephen's African Methodist Episcopal in Chicago founded Provident Hospital (Bagley & Carroll, 1995).

Currently churches serving African Americans continue to act as a healing force for African-American families. However, the nature of support and service has changed in response to current needs. For example, a New York congregation holds city-wide oratorical and essay contests for children to promote education; while a Chicago church offers health screening for hypertension and diabetes along with health education and exercise programs for senior citizens (Bagley & Carroll, 1995).

The contemporary church exists within many variations, including the historically Black Protestant denominations, to the Black divisions of what might be considered White denominations, to the Black Muslims. All of these church communities have responded differently to the same obstacles which influence African-American communities (McAdoo & Crawford, 1991). Most often, churches represent a valuable resource for families facing crisis. Furthermore, churches frequently provide assistance beyond that which is considered crisis management (McAdoo & Crawford, 1991). McAdoo and Crawford (1991) state that churches have always contributed to positive mental health.

Depending on the church and the needs of the community where it resides, these contributions may be quite diverse. Many churches provide a large number of youth role models. In the author's own Likert scale survey research (1995) 44% of social workers indicated that "many" or "most" of the low-income, urban, African-American families with whom they work find positive family role models within churches. A significant portion of many African-American church communities consist of elderly individuals. Here, they receive respect and caring that promotes a sense of family as they grow older (Boyd-Franklin, 1989). These churches have offered a source of affirmation of psychological striving for a sense of self-esteem. In addition, churches have preserved culture and heritage and have acted as an agent for social change (Billingsley, 1989).

In the midst of the identified strengths, the church has played a particularly large role in its provision of youth programs and religious education. Yet, the church's contributions to mental health extend beyond the value of service. The church provides individuals with the opportunity for service and gives membership opportunities for leadership and status positions (McAdoo & Crawford, 1991). The church offers women and men opportunities for authority and leadership which are non-existent outside of the Church. Early on, Mays and Nicholson (1933) cited the church as the only institution that is owned, managed, supported and patronized by African-Americans. Often, volunteers lead the programs, and women play a primary role in program maintenance (Billingsley, 1989). Volunteer programs which have acted as a powerful source of family support. Within these programs, African-American women have derived significant benefits. This is particularly true for women who have felt the impact of high levels of unemployment. Under this condition, more than half of these women raise children without spousal support, and are therefore under a tremendous stress (McAdoo, 1989). To deal with issues even more complex than this one, churches have been forced to overcome traditional reluctance, and thus, to meet the challenge of addressing issues such as sexuality, conception, and drugs. For some churches, theological and religious conflict exists, and areas such as these present a difficult and delicate issue (Lewin, 1988). Although there have been theological roadblocks to addressing these issues for some churches, other African-American churches offer programs to reduce teen pregnancy, keep children in school, provide role models, and find adoptive homes for African-American infants (McAdoo & Crawford, 1991).

One example of an African-American Church program which provides family support is illustrated through the Congress of National Black Churches (CNBC) and Project Spirit. This program demonstrates some basic concepts and ideas which may be implemented to support African-American families in therapy (McAdoo & Crawford, 1991). In addition, programs such as this may be used as a resource or referral to meet specific needs of these families in addition to therapy.

Social service professionals may want to work closely with African-American church communities especially with those congregations to which their clients belong. Family therapists may also want to work closely with clergy and church leaders. When doing this, therapists must recognize that the role clergy may play is not simply as a referral source. First, clergy, being someone whom the family trusts may assure the family that therapy is safe, and that their religious and other beliefs will be respected. This may be done verbally and by the presence of clergy in therapy sessions. This technique would be helpful in building rapport

61

and trust with African-American families who have reason to be skeptical of mental health agencies. For religious families who value self-sufficiency, clergy may provide the support services or concrete needs which would be helpful to the family. Clergy may also provide support so that the family is comfortable seeking and attaining needed services. In this way, clergy might assure the family that it is "acceptable" to utilize various services such as welfare.

The religious organization which has been cited, the CNBC, consists of six predominantly African-American denominations including African Methodist Episcopal, Christian Methodist Episcopal, Church of God in Christ, National Baptist Convention of America, Inc., National Missionary Baptist Convention of America, and the Progressive National Baptist Convention, Inc. This organization, being voluntary and non-profit, strives to promote charity and fellowship among members of the congregations. Through this program, the denominations have come together to provide services which would not be possible of one denomination to provide alone. These institutions have begun to offer family support to members as well as the community at large. Such support services have an important impact on current community problems. The programs of this organization, called Project SPIRIT, are available to the wider community in churches in Oakland, Atlanta, Indianapolis, and Washington, D.C. The programs include three parts: parent education, involving parents from the community; pastoral counseling education for seminarians and in-service training for pastors and clergy; and after-school, tutorial, coping skills development, and ethnic education programs for 6 to 12 year-old children (Mc Adoo & Crawford, 1991).

Funded primarily by the Carnegie Foundation and the Lilly Endowment, church volunteers and families run the program. In the largest of the three programs, the after-school program, transportation is provided to the children participating. Forty-five minutes is spent doing homework; and living skills, African-American history, and coping skills, then occupies the next two hours. For the most part, children do not have parents at home waiting for them. Thus, the program provides them with a safe secure place while parents work. Families in the programs primarily faced two problems: poverty and parenting alone. Half of the participants were married and half were females parenting without a husband. Fifty-five percent of the families were at or below the $14,000 poverty level for a family of four (Washington Post, 1988).

Spirituality

Contemporary scholars such as Nobles (1972, 1980), Baldwin (1985), and Asante (1988) have identified an Afrocentric approach to philosophy and human behavior which is incorporated into the concept known as the African-American paradigm. According to the African American paradigm, humanity is perceived as collective rather individual. African-Americans express this collective view as shared concern and responsibility for others' well-being (Ak'bar, 1984; Ho, 1987; Houston, 1990; Schiele, 1990). This spirit of the collective has been expressed by the fact that African-Americans did not have words for "alone" and ownership at the time of initial contact with Caucasians (Daly, Jennings, Beckett, & Leashore, 1995). This paradigm recognizes feelings and emotions in addition to rational and logical ways of thinking. Materialism and competition are replaced with spiritual awareness and cooperation (Ak'bar, 1984; Baldwin, 1985; Ho, 1987; Turner, 1991). In the authors' Likert scale research, only 4% of social workers and therapists currently working with low-income, urban African-American families reported that "most" of the low-income, urban, African-American families with whom they work valued competition. In addition, only 4% reported that "most" of the low-income, urban, African-American families whom they work with have family members who pursue their own needs over those of the family (1995).

From the perspective of the African-American paradigm, one can understand the impact of African heritage as well as the experience of racism, oppression and discrimination (Everett, Chipungu, & Leashore, 1991). This perspective identifies positive aspects of African-American life which are

63

embedded in spirituality and a worldview that recognizes African-American traits and commitment to common causes (Grier & Cobb, 1968; Hill, 1971; Houston, 1990; Nobles, 1972, 1980; & Miller, 1992). Traditionally, friendship, compassion, sharing, honesty, courage, and self-control are virtues which are to be upheld in African communities; while cheating, greed, and vices are to be quickly addressed and corrected (Houston, 1990; Khoapa, 1980; Mbiti, 1969; Menkiti, 1984; & Turner, 1991). African society promotes social structures and organizations which include all members in mutual sharing and responsibility for others. Although emphasis on the interpersonal and sharing kinship beyond blood ties resembles socialism (Houston, 1990), Khoapa (1980) differentiated African socialism from European Marxist socialism stating that African socialism focuses on universal charity and conduct codes that give dignity to all people regardless of their station in life; unlike Marxist societies which view citizens as belonging to the state. Thus, the Marxist perspective centralizes planning with little input from lower level workers.

Recognition of African values and the feeling of being unique and of historic merit relates to spirituality as it fosters some sense of connectedness on an individual as well as on a collective level. From a strength or resiliency perspective, one might say that the Black Church inspired African-Americans to view themselves as descendants from a great people because of race and color (Bagley & Carroll, 1995).

According to Beverly, African-American spirituality is both offensive and defensive (Beverly, 1995). African-American spirituality is defensive since it acts as a rebuttal to the world's offensive behaviors directed toward people of color. African-American spirituality acts as offensive because it serves as a proactive framework which allows African-Americans to see past the contingencies of today. Although African-American spirituality is invisible as a force, it becomes visible in all products of African-American life. From an offensive/defensive perspective, spirituality acts as both a protective as well as a strengthening force.

For African-Americans, Beverly describes the role of spirituality as consisting of **objective reality** and **subjective interpretation**. To begin, people of African descent experience an objective reality which includes personal devaluation, social injustice, societal inconsistency, and personal impotence (Chestang, 1972). As individuals internalize this objective reality, subjective interpretation occurs, and results in Black rage (Grier & Cobbs, 1980). Depending on how this rage is processed, it can lead to severe states of dysfunction or a transcendent state of mental health. Here, the key lies in the filter through which it is processed. When filtered through an African-American spiritual funnel, the probable outcome is positive mental health; if not, mental illness or other self-defeating behaviors are likely to occur (Beverly, 1995). The difficulty African-Americans have in filtering their rage through a spiritual funnel results from the underdevelopment of one's spiritual domain of existence. This domain lies in all African-Americans, but like all other aspects of living, it must be acknowledged, nurtured, and developed (Beverly, 1995, p. 22). When African-Americans seek to define their personhood, worthiness, and validation through Eurocentric paradigms, mental illness and social dysfunction prove inevitable. Often, their presence in mental health systems is marked by the dilemma of seeking validation from an invalidating society. Those African-Americans who develop their spiritual domains are able to overcome this dilemma (1995).

Dr. Wade Nobles, clinical psychologist at San Francisco University, argued that all African-Americans need to know what already lies within them. In his speech at the University of Michigan, entitled "African Psychologic Illumination of the Spirit," Nobles stated "We've got to get back to the spirit." Here, he referred to "Sakhu", an African word meaning spirit was well as a practice dating back to the fifteenth century. It covers a collection of religious and psychological teachings focused on mediation and the importance of the spirit in relation to having a healthy mind and body (Beverly, 1995).

As previously discussed, the Black Church has historically provided social, economic and emotional support for African American families at times when services from mainstream social institutions were unavailable to them. The following case illustration shows how support from the Black Church assisted the client in working toward the goals and objectives specified in her service plan.

Case Illustration:

Ms. Rhonda Sims is a 28 year-old single African American mother of six children who was referred to her local community mental health center for Adult Outpatient services by Ms. Clare, the Sunday school teacher at her non-denominational church. Ms. Clare noticed that Ms. Sims often looked tired when attending services. Ms. Sims' two youngest children, Larry, 3 years-old, and Amelia, 5 years-old attend Ms. Clare's Sunday school program. Ms. Clare noticed that often Ms. Sims looked exhausted when she brought the children to Sunday classes. The children were often irritable, and there were times when they seemed to defy many of Ms. Sims' directives. There was one Sunday when Ms. Sims called Larry to come with her and the other children. After Larry ignored her for a few minutes, Ms. Sims attempted to pick him up and he began calling her names and hitting her. Ms. Sims became extremely upset. She told her oldest child, Lyn, to watch the other children, and that she would return.

That afternoon Ms. Sims was tearful as she confided to Ms. Clare that she often felt embarrassed, "when the children don't listen, and all the other mothers look at me like I'm a bad mom." Ms. Sims went on to say that the other parents did not seem to understand what it was like for her to be caring for her six children with little support. Ms. Sims explained that she often felt helpless and hopeless, and there were some nights that she could not sleep. Ms. Clare expressed concern for Ms. Sims, and she asked Ms. Sims if family therapy might be helpful. Ms. Sims replied that she would think about it, and Ms. Clare noticed she seemed hesitant.

A few weeks later, Ms. Sims felt overwhelmed. She had not attended Church for the past few weeks, and she was beginning to feel alone and isolated. It seemed that she was no longer reading or roller-skating with the children as it

66

was a struggle for her to find the energy to motivate herself. She worried that she could not be a good mother to the children if she did not get help. Although Ms. Sims was skeptical, she trusted Ms. Clare. Ms. Sims called Ms. Clare and asked her if she could meet with her after the next Sunday mass. At this time, Ms. Clare gave Ms. Sims the support and information she needed about the services offered at the nearby community mental health agency.

Ms. Sims met with Ms. Bonds, an adult therapist, for an intake and information gathering session. As Ms. Bonds inquired about Ms. Sims' family, work and personal life, she obtained information that would be useful in assisting Ms. Sims with the development of her service plan. Since Ms. Sims reported that the reason that she came to the community mental health agency was because she felt hopeless and helpless about her life, Ms. Bonds decided that it would be important to closely examine the various activities which were part of Ms. Sim's life at this time and in the past.

As she conducted the initial interview, Ms. Bonds remembered to ask questions about spirituality, church attendance and religion. Ms. Sims seemed comfortable answering these questions, and she seemed impressed that Ms. Bonds was interested in hearing about how important her religion and Church were to her. Ms. Sims stated, "I didn't think that a therapist would include these kinds of things in an assessment, but my Church is a really important part of my life so I guess it makes perfect sense." Ms. Sims went on to explain that when her divorce became final about six months ago, she did not feel comfortable in the Baptist Church which she had attended for 15 years because since many of the Church members publicly voiced disapproval of her divorce. "I was so afraid and alone, but I had to have something to pull me through this difficult time. Church and prayer have always been important to me, so I decided to look for a Church community that promoted values and ideas that were similar to my own. One summer day, the children and I were exhausted and hungry, and I saw a flier in the store that said that the non-denominational church nearby was sponsoring a free lunch program. I walked there with the children. The people there were very kind. We were able to relax and eat. I, myself, enjoyed the adult company and Ms. Clare, the Sunday school teacher, really helped me to keep the children under control. Right now, Ms. Clare is my adult friend. "

Ms. Sims added that her new Church had also provided her with clothing for herself and the children and that the family had been chosen for the "Adopt-a-Family " program in which Church volunteers provided holiday gifts and food for a family in need. Ms. Sims stated that, for her, the Church provided peace as well as a sense of family and community.

As she began work with Ms. Sims and her family, Ms. Bonds continued to incorporate the Church and Ms. Sims' religion into her service plan. Ms. Bonds diagnosed Ms. Sims with Adjustment Disorder with Depressed Mood and included a rule out for major Depression. Ms. Bonds identified Ms. Sims' exploration and expression of her spirituality as a strength. Ms. Bonds further noted that Ms. Sims had creatively used the time spent with her Church community as a way to cope with feelings of hopelessness and helplessness. Ms. Bonds thought that it was significant the Ms. Sims met her "one adult friend " at Church.

It was also important for Ms. Bonds to consider the means by which Ms. Sims became connected to her new Church. The free lunch program provided a concrete need for Ms. Sims and her family. Since Ms. Sims was living on a limited income, and caring for her six children, the offer of a free lunch was attractive. In addition, Ms. Sims felt that the people she met were accepting and non-judgmental. Although Ms. Sims continued to feel overwhelmed, hopeless and helpless at times, her participation in being a part of this Church community seemed to provide an important coping mechanism for her.

As Ms. Bonds and Ms. Sims developed a service plan, Ms. Sims stated she wanted to feel worthwhile and successful again. Ms. Bonds and Ms. Sims decided that for Ms. Sims to feel worthwhile and successful, she would have to find positive coping skills to deal with her feelings of hopelessness and helplessness.

When Ms. Bonds further explored coping skills with Ms. Sims, Ms. Sims reported that the Church community had helped her through a difficult time in her life and that she would like to continue to use this support as a coping skill. Ms. Sims stated that having more friends might help her to cope, because she would have someone to talk to. Ms. Sims also mentioned that she heard about a parenting support group that was being offered at the Church.

Based on this information, Ms. Sims and Ms. Bonds decided that Ms. Sims would begin to work toward one primary goal using two objectives to help her to achieve this goal. The primary goal identified was: Ms. Sims will report consistent use of positive coping skills to deal with feelings of hopelessness and helplessness. Objectives included: 1) Ms. Sims will make at least 2 new friends within the next three months; and 2) Ms. Sims will participate in the parenting support group and discuss new effective parenting techniques during at least five sessions.

For Ms. Sims, both of these objectives could be achieved through participation in Church activities. Ms. Bonds also told Ms. Sims that Ms. Clare seemed to play an important role in her life, and that Ms. Clare was welcome to attend sessions. With a smile, Ms. Sims said she would appreciate that.

In this case, the Church provided temporary child care, food and other concrete resources that Ms. Sims may have felt uncomfortable obtaining from social service agencies. As earlier stated, Black families turned to their Church communities when various social and material services were unavailable to them. Thus, it may be helpful for social workers and case managers to develop strong relationships with community churches so that they may link their consumers with various resources. In addition, the Church community provided Ms. Sims and her children with a place of comfort and peace. For Ms. Sims, it was also a place to make friends and gain the emotional support needed to overcome the struggles of her daily life.

Knowledge Framework Component 5: Trauma, Grief and Loss

Trauma, grief, and loss seem to have a significant influence on the lives of many low-income, urban, Africa-American families. Like the other framework components, the exploration of this component also shows various strengths which are present in these families. Strengths are reflected in the families' ability to cope and survive after the actual traumatic event. Trauma, grief and loss may be experienced on various levels: individual, family, group and community. Often, children are the most adversely affected by the trauma, grief, and loss often present in low-income, urban communities. Social workers and family therapists need to increase their awareness of the trauma, grief and loss experienced within the low-income, urban, African-American families whom they serve. It is important to define trauma and to understand the stressful events which precipitate the feelings of grief and loss. Furthermore, it is important to understand what this means for low-income, urban, African-American families.

First, the feelings of grief and loss may be caused by external stresses on an individual family member such as a crisis on a father's job, an act of violence which occurs at a child's school, or the death of a mother's close friend. External stress can also directly affect the whole family. Examples of this include events such as the family house burning down, a financial crisis which prompts the family to apply for public assistance; or the murder of an immediate family member (Woods & Hollis, 1990). The fear of change which is present after a traumatic event produces feelings of bereavement, grief and loss. The experience is often profound as familiar relationships must be changed and modified. For most families, a period of disorganization and confusion follows the traumatic event. The external stresses which have been described may be commonly known as crises. A crisis may be identified as any major event which involves change and causes individuals and families to restructure ways in which they view themselves, their environment, and their way of life (Woods & Hollis, 1990, p. 427). When one experiences a great deal of stress due to a specific event, severe anxiety often

71

produces symptoms which interfere with working through the situation and reaching a point of resolution (First, 1994). For children, the ability to think in an abstract manner and thus resolve the feelings of grief and loss is not present, and thus, resolution may not occur until later years. An extreme response to a stressor may produce Posttraumatic Stress Disorder (PTSD). Symptoms may reflect anxiety, avoidance of stimuli associated with the traumatic event, a restriction of emotional expression, nightmares, an exaggerated startle response, and a host of other symptoms (First, 1994). PTSD includes a presumed etiology, a directly experienced or witnessed traumatic event involving death, or a threat of death or serious injury (First, 1994;). The severity of the disorder increases according to the severity of the traumatic event (First, 1994). In the author's research, 92% of the participants (social workers, therapists, and case managers who worked primarily with low-income, urban, African American families) indicated that "many" or "most" of the families with whom they worked experienced significant trauma or loss and were seeking to resolve grief and loss issues. As one might assume, violent acts often lead to trauma, grief and loss for low-income, urban African American families. For social workers and therapists who help low-income, urban African American families to overcome the adverse affects of traumatic events, the challenge is to increase one's personal understanding of the many forces which influence African American families living in the inner-cities.

As one becomes more familiar with urban life, it becomes easier to relate to the "challenge" as it has been spoken and written about by Alex Kotlowitz (1995), a journalist who writes extensively on urban affairs, children and the inner-city. He describes the "challenge" as learning ". . . to understand the chasm, ... to understand the forces at work on the lives of the children, to recognize their strengths as well as their frailties, and to put a human face on the people living in these communities. " To begin to understand trauma, grief and loss and the levels on which it influences low-income, urban, African-American families, it is important to first recognize traumatic events which occur in the home and to examine how these events have influenced the family as a group as well as individual family members. The author interviewed and surveyed workers who worked primarily with the identified population. Forty-eight percent of these participants reported that "many" or "most" of the families with whom they worked had experienced trauma, grief, or loss; and 44% of the respondents reported that "most" of the families with whom they served had experienced some form of trauma, grief, or loss. When participants in the same study were asked to elaborate on issues important to low-income, African-American families, 60% of the respondents described issues related to trauma, grief and loss. Traumatic experiences described by these professionals included domestic violence, including physical and sexual maltreatment of children in the home; the death of a parent or close family member; homelessness; and witnessing violent crimes such as rapes, murders and assaults.

With regard to trauma which occurs in the home, the issue of domestic violence is found in all socioeconomic, gender, racial and ethnic groups; yet limited attention is given to its dynamics among African-American families (Daly, Jennings, Beckett, & Leashore, 1995). The available literature indicates that African-American women cope with domestic violence differently than Caucasian women. African-American women who experienced domestic violence seemed to be especially sensitive to family and social support systems. In addition, social supports such as extended family, the presence of a non-nuclear family member in the home, or a long-time residence in a neighborhood seemed to reduce the number of spouse assaults among African-Americans (Cooley & Beckett, 1988). Research also indicated that African-Americans and Caucasian women used the same range of services; but African-American women were more hesitant than Caucasian women to use some specific services. For example, African-American women rarely used shelter services, but were more likely to use medical services, a service least likely to be used among Caucasian women. Caucasian women were also more likely to seek mental health services; while African-American women

73

were unlikely to use counseling services. Literature has suggested that, for African-American women, mental health services may conflict with their cultural experience and may be inadequate to meet their needs (Bingham & Guinyard, 1982).

It is important to note that many African-American women perceive battering experiences differently than Caucasian women (Beckett & Cooley, 1987; Richie, 1981; Vontress, 1973). African-American women tend to be more likely to view physical abuse from the perspective of racial and sexual oppression. Rather than simply viewing domestic violence entirely in individual, family or power terms some African-American women may be likely to view battering as the result of African-American males' displaced anger and aggression. In this way the African-American males' battering is seen as a response to racism and the ongoing struggle to assume or maintain economic and other social roles which are typically expected of African-American males.

For African-American women and families who experience domestic violence, the African-American community provides supportive structure. The specific process of this support has yet to be well-documented in literature, but it is clear that family, neighbors, and the community provide advice, counseling, and shelter and that such support has eased family problems. This type of assistance is consistent with the African-American value of the extended family and the helping tradition previously discussed. For social workers and family therapists, working with these families, this type of collective aid should be viewed as a strength (Daly, Jennings, Beckett, & Leashore, 1995). It should be noted that domestic violence is one of the many situations in which extended family serves as a helpful support to African-Americans.

For African-American families living in the inner-cities, support from the extended family as it serves to help the family deal with issues such as domestic violence, is only one example of resilience. Yet, the concept of resilience must be perceived in terms of the cultural context; and the socioeconomic and

74

environmental context in which culture plays a role. Often it is the children who are at great risk of suffering from trauma, grief and loss as many of those living in ghettos grow up seeing a different kind of culture emerging, one marked by violence, abuse, despair, and diminished hope (McCubbin, Futrell, Thompson, & Thompson, 1995). Traditionally, African-American families have demonstrated a strong sense of community (Daly, Jennings, Beckett, & Leashore, 1995). However, for extremely impoverished African-American families who live in urban areas which are often unsafe, this sense of community may be jeopardized. After observing a low-income Chicago neighborhood for two years, Alex Kotlowitz concluded that the construct of community in this area was minimal. He observed the community lacked trust among its members, had weak institutions, non-functional political organization, disconnected churches and only three social service agencies (Kotlowitz, 1995).

The forces acting on these families living in extremely impoverished communities break down the strong sense of community and helping traditions which would otherwise be present. One of the most powerful forces is violence. Kolowitz states: "As we prosper as a nation, a group of us is residing in neighborhoods which I believe to be among the worst to grow up in in the world, (1995, p. 5). According to the authors' research, 52% of the workers surveyed reported that few of the low-income urban African-American families with whom they work live in safe areas (1995). Like many others, Kotlowitz reported that he was unprepared for the intensity and the severe nature of the brutality which he encountered (1995).

Although the violence itself is traumatic, its aftermath proves even more devastating. Kotlowitz (1995) noticed that children who had witnessed the violent death of a friend or relative displayed Posttraumatic Stress Disorder symptoms which were the same as those displayed by veterans returning from war. These symptoms included hyperactivity, aggression, violent acting out; depression and sleeplessness (First, 1994). In addition, children experienced physiological problems such as headaches and stomach aches (Kotlowitz, 1995). Another possible result of children living in violent communities is that children may be conditioned to commit violent crimes. Gibb (1989) has asserted that African-American adolescents are analogous to an endangered species. These youth have been mishandled by the juvenile justice system; and mislabeled, ignored, or excluded from many mental health systems. These experiences, combined with the limited social economic resources, support the idea that African-American youth are exposed to unique risk factors which influence their growth and development (Rickely & Allen, 1987; Simons & Gray, 1989; Spencer, Cole, Dupree, Glymph & Pierre, 1993; & McAdoo, 1995). Recently, there has been a call for research focusing on understanding African-American youth in terms of African-American norms rather than mainstream and traditional models of development (Barbarin, 1993; Jones, 1994; & Piatt et al, 1993). Myers (1989) stated that these youth face a reality quite different from that other youth. Thus, these youth must develop coping mechanisms to deal with the various stressors using limited resources. In order to meet the mental health needs of low-income African-American youth, Myers suggests using a mental health model which examines the stress and unique coping strategies which are often utilized by these youth (1989). This approach is consistent with the strength and resilience model which has been discussed as the first framework component.

Research focusing on the developmental pathways of African-American youth compared to those of Caucasian youth noted a distinction with respect to the youth's display of aggressive acts (Loeber et al, 1993). African-American youth were more likely to begin their sequence of aggressive behavior with fighting or gang-like fighting; while Caucasian youth tended to begin their sequence earlier by engaging in disruptive behavior such as annoying or bullying before engaging in actual fighting.

It is important to consider the types of traumatic events which are experienced by low income urban African-American families. As previously discussed, the issue of violence is significant. It has been stated that Black youths are suffering from epidemic rates of violent crimes as they die from violence and enter the juvenile justice system at several times the rate of their Caucasian peers (Children's Defense Fund, 1993). Black children are also more likely than White children to be the victims of violent crime. Black children are three to ten times more likely to be victims of violent crime depending on their age and gender. Furthermore, homicide is the leading cause of death among black youth, ages 18 to 24. When compared to White children, Black children and adolescents of all ages are more likely to die as a result of firearms. Black males in their teens were three and four times more likely than White peers to be victims of handgun crimes during the period of 1979 to 1987 (Children's Defense Fund, 1993). Violence has also become evident in urban school environments as two out of five Black male high school students reported carrying a weapon in the past month; and more than half of these youth reported carrying a firearm in 1990 (Children's Defense Fund, 1993). In addition, Black youths were more than five times as likely as their White counterparts to report being arrested for committing a violent crime in 1990. Nationwide, the number of Black youths in custody has increased by 30% between 1985 and 1989; Black youth represented 42% of the youths in public juvenile facilities on a one-day count in 1989 (Children's Defense Fund, 1993). Based on these facts, the issue of violence has influenced many Black youth and their families. Often the parents of these youth also have experienced violence and thus, these parents may have unresolved issues regarding trauma, grief and loss. Social workers who serve these families should thus demonstrate awareness of the various influence of violence on Black communities, families, and individuals. As previously discussed, the influence of violence on the Black individual may be seen in PTSD symptoms. The feelings of distrust which Kotlowitz has explored, may become evident in work with Black families who have experienced violence (1995). For example, an adolescent may state that he/she does not have friends but rather, associates, since friends cannot be trusted (Kotlowitz, 1995).

77

It is also important to remember that traumatic events do not necessarily have to be violent events. Many times the separation from a biological family member may be traumatic. Another traumatic experience includes living in an impoverished home or neighborhood. According to the information from the Children's Defense Fund, more than half of all Black children live with only one parent (1993). When compared to their White peers, Black children were three times more likely to live in public housing (Children's Defense Fund, 1993). Almost three in ten poor Black homes had physical problems with their house; and almost one in five poor Black homes were reported to have cracks, inside holes, or signs of rats. One in eight low-income African-American families reported lack of heat at least once during the winter (Children's Defense Fund, 1993). The following case illustration demonstrates various techniques which may be used to assist low-income, urban, African-American families as they cope with trauma, grief and loss.

Case Illustration:

The Simons requested mental health services because of 8 year-old Toya's aggressiveness in her current foster home. Toya had two younger brothers, an older sister, and three younger sisters. Toya and her 10 year-old sister were placed with their Aunt Libby because their mother's boyfriend had been extremely abusive to the children and their mother, Gloria. Toya's other siblings were in other foster care placements; and Toya's oldest sister was placed in a residential home. Toya's mother, Gloria, had a history of substance abuse, and was abusing cocaine and alcohol at the time the children were taken from the home. Toya had also witnessed friends of the family being beaten and shot outside the family home.

Toya's Aunt Libby became concerned when Toya stated that, "I don't want to live this way. I want to die." During the first interview, the therapist, Ms. Kline, gathered information from the foster care worker, Ms. Bauer; Toya; Laverne, Toya's 10 year-old sister; and Aunt Libby. Ms. Kline noticed immediately that Toya was fidgety. Times when she did not have Ms. Kline's full

78

attention were especially difficult for Toya. Toya often interrupted the other family members and Ms. Bauer when they were talking with Ms. Kline. Ms. Kline commented that she was glad that Toya had much to tell her and she told Toya that she did not want to miss anything that Toya had to say. Thus, she gave Toya a pencil and colored markers and told her that when she thought of something she wanted to say, she could either write it down or draw a picture that reminded her of it so that she could tell Ms. Kline when it was her turn to talk. At times, Toya wrote and drew frantically as if she might forget something. Toya seemed glad that she found someone who would listen to her story. When Ms. Kline told Toya that she could play with the toys, she moved quickly from one task to another. Ms. Kline gently reminded Toya to pick up one toy before starting to play with another. Ms. Kline observed which toys Toya liked and she began building rapport with Toya by asking her questions about her favorite activities, foods and people. Toya reported that she enjoyed drawing and writing on paper and on chalkboards; playing in the water, and going to the store. She reported that her favorite foods were greens and pizza. When talking about her favorite people, Toya stated that she liked her oldest sister, Kim, 14; and her mother best. "I get along with them best, and I'm mad because I can't be with them. They sent Kim to some home because she was being bad, I guess, but she was nice to me. I haven't seen my mom in two weeks. Ms. Bauer says I can see her soon, and we can visit, but I'm not sure that I believe her." Toya added that she did not like Larry, her mother's boyfriend stating that, "He's bad. He was so mean to us, and he had a lot of bad friends, too." At this point, Ms. Bauer reassured Toya that Larry was in jail. and the he could not hurt her or her family anymore. Toya responded by stating that his friends were still around and that he might get his friends to hurt her mom. Ms. Kline picked up on Toya's concern for her mother. Ms. Kline's most primary concern was Toya's statement that she wanted to die; and thus, Ms. Kline spent time talking with Toya about this issue:

Ms. Kline: All of us here are worried about you, Toya.

79

Toya: (Smiling)	Why?
Ms. Bauer:	We're worried because of the things that you have been saying and doing. You seem very unhappy, and you have had a hard time lately.
Ms. Kline:	Toya, do you understand why you came here today?
Toya:	'Cause I say I want to kill myself?' (Still smiling)
Ms. Kline:	Well, yes. That's a big part of why you are here today. When you say things like that, you make us feel concerned about you. None of us want you to die. You seem like a nice little girl and I don't want you to die. You are here to get help so that you can talk about what is making you feel so bad that you would say that you want to kill yourself.
Toya:	**You** don't want me to die?
Ms. Kline:	Of course not. I don't want to see children die. What's making you feel so bad, Toya?
Toya:	Larry. I wrote you a lot of notes about him. (Toya begins to show Ms. Kline various drawings and notes. Toya first pointed to a picture.) This is Larry and my mom. He is yelling that he wants to kill her. This is another picture of Larry telling me to hit Laverne. He is yelling so loud. Now Laverne doesn't like me, but I was afraid that if I didn't do what he said, he would hurt me.
Ms. Kline:	You are really afraid of Larry. He sounds really scary.
Toya:	He is; and he's bad. If you don't believe me, here's his phone number. (Toya unfolds another piece of paper with numbers on it). Call him and see.
Ms. Kline:	I believe you, Toya. Do you believe her, Ms. Bauer?
Ms. Bauer:	Oh, yes, I believe her. A lot of people believe her. That's
why Larry is in jail.	

80

(Ms. Kline asked Laverne and Toya's Aunt Libby if they believed Toya, and both answered, yes.)

Ms. Kline asked the others present if she could spend some individual time with Toya. Toya seemed to become more and more comfortable with Ms. Kline as they talked. Ms. Kline noticed that Toya was having trouble sitting still, so she told Toya that she could use the chalkboard to draw pictures as they talked; and Toya responded immediately by going to the chalkboard and drawing pictures of Larry and some of the "mean things that he did to us." Toya drew one picture which she described as "the time that Larry tried to burn our house down, and he started a fire in the living room." In another, Toya's mom was backing away, and Larry had a knife. Ms. Kline also asked Toya to draw a picture of her family. Toya drew Kim first, and then she drew her mother, followed by the rest of her siblings. She added her Aunt Libby, and her cousin, Jerome at the end. Ms. Kline then asked Toya to sit down and she stated that there was something very important that she had to talk to Toya about before Toya left today. Ms. Kline addressed Toya's statement that she wanted to kill herself. In response, Toya expressed a great deal of worry that Larry might hurt her mother or her other siblings or send his friends to hurt them. Toya stated that she had never tried to kill herself, and she did not have a plan to do so; but she felt so scared that she just wanted to give up sometimes. Ms. Kline told Toya that she wanted to work with her so that Toya could begin to feel happier during this difficult time in her life. Toya stated that she really did not want to kill herself, but there were times when she did not know what else to say or do. Ms. Kline responded by telling Toya that she, Toya's family members, and Ms. Bauer would help her to find ways to cope.

Ms. Kline then brought Toya's family members and Ms. Bauer in the room. The rest of this initial session focused on helping Toya to find coping skills. Toya was able to explain to Aunt Libby, Laverne and Ms. Bauer that she didn't really want to die, she felt confused, scared and afraid; she "said that" she really did not know what else to do. Laverne shared that she also felt afraid, confused, and sad;

81

so Ms. Kline chose to utilize Laverne's statement, and she asked Laverne how she handled these feelings. Laverne stated that she talked to her Aunt Libby, often before she went to bed; and she wrote in a journal, especially when she felt sad. The family and Ms. Bauer participated in helping Toya to find coping skills which she could use at least until her next session.

Ms. Kline:	You seem so worried and scared for your mom, Toya. What can we do to help you with that?
Toya:	Well, I know it would make things worse for everyone if I died, so I know that I cannot do that. It would help if I just knew that my mom was O.K. I can try to do some of the things that Laverne does to help herself, but I still won't know for sure that my mom is O.K.
Ms. Kline:	Maybe Ms. Bauer can help you to connect with your mother, Toya. Why don't you ask her?
Toya:	Can you help me? (Turning to Ms. Bauer).
Ms. Bauer:	I am trying to arrange for you to visit with your mother right now, Toya. You should be able to see your mother in about a week. Right now, I can give you the phone number where you can reach your mom and you can call her so that you know that she is safe.

This initial interview ended with Ms. Kline initiating an agreement between Toya, herself, Ms. Bauer, Laverne and Aunt Libby. Aunt Libby agreed to let Toya call her mother every other night. Aunt Libby also explained to Toya that her Mother was in a drug rehabilitation program, and that she was safe and getting help. Ms. Bauer agreed to call Toya and Laverne on the next day to give them an exact time when they would be able to visit with their mother. Laverne agreed that she would teach Toya about how to use a journal. Ms. Kline made an appointment with the family, and she told Toya that she would be looking forward to hearing about any of the coping skills which worked for her.

Case Illustration Assessment

Ms. Kline diagnosed Toya with Posttraumatic Stress Disorder (PTSD), 309.81 (First, 1994) due to the nature of Toya's presenting issue. The traumatic events which Toya had been exposed to included her separation from her mother; her witness to her mother's abuse by Larry; and Larry's physical abuse to her. Toya presented with many PTSD symptoms. Toya's play, for example, included themes related to the trauma which she had suffered. Her pictures drawn both on the paper and on the chalkboard seemed to represent her own way of communicating with the therapist the events she had witnessed. Her statement that she wanted to die told Ms. Kline that Toya's fear gave her the sense of a foreshortened future, another PTSD symptom; and Toya's fidgeting and hypervigilance were also typical symptoms.

Toya seemed to have responded well to Ms. Kline's statement that she believed Toya. In this way, Ms. Kline used a technique suggested by Alex Kotlowitz, the idea of breaking the silence. The "silence" was also broken as Ms. Kline spent individual time with Toya and while she allowed Toya to tell her about the traumatic events she had witnessed by drawing on the chalkboard, writing, and drawing on paper. In later sessions, these techniques could be further developed and used as coping skills. Thus, Toya's service plan would focus on the development of positive coping skills to help her to deal with her feelings, and thoughts related to the trauma, grief and loss which she had experienced. Ms. Kline planned to develop close relationships with Toya's family members, including her mother; and Ms. Bauer, Toya's foster care worker. Ms. Kline also planned to talk with school professionals in order to assist in providing an environment which was supportive of Toya's development of positive coping skills and emphatic to her situation. As previously suggested, developing close relationships with community agencies will help to maximize resources available to clients and their families.

83

Chapter III: Interventions to Help More Low Income African-American Families Toward Positive Change

Counseling low-income urban African-American families presents an array of challenges derived from the social, political and economic environments in which families struggle for survival. In addition, these families are confronted with multiple barriers imposed by racism and discrimination. Helping families within this context first involves gaining their trust in the engagement process.

Engaging Families in Treatment - Understanding the Family's Frame of Reference

An initial task in working with low income, African-American families is engagement in which the therapist and family jointly explore the nature of the relationship leading to a development of a mutual contract and expectations of what the treatment process will entail. An important attribute of engagement is understanding the family's frame of reference. Wright, Salleby and Lecca (1983) suggest it is necessary to adapt a transcultural perspective to accomplish this. They identify a number of basic assumptions of a transcultural perspective, several of these which were of particular significance in assembling the practice framework discussed in this chapter. These are 1) "The organization and methodologies of helping are value-laden." 2) "All aspects of the helping process are infused with cultural symbols, knowledge and culturally patterned activity." 3) "Cultural sensitivity, awareness, experiential recognition and affirmation of the cultural factor must precede competent helping of ethnic minorities" (Wright, 1983, p. 22). A similar position is advocated by Gaw (1982) and Lum (1986). Both writers suggest that workers need to develop an understanding of ethnic frame of reference and values if practice is to be ethnic sensitive. Similarly, McGoldrick, Pearce and Giordano (1982) propose that problems can neither be diagnosed nor treated without understanding the frame of reference of the person seeking help. To understand a religious family's frame of reference workers should obtain answers to the following questions regarding the client's definition of the problem; the client's perceived solutions to the problem; current places or people to whom the client turns to for help; family patterns; ways that the family deals with life transitions; and challenges present for a therapist of the same or a different background (Mc Goldrick, p.XV, 1989). Wright, et al also suggest a paradigm for understanding the frame of reference of an ethnic minority family. Wright's paradigm has four components which are viewed as systems. System 1 is comprised of social relationships and association which relates to social norms, rules, expectations and roles which make manageable and predictable the complexity of relationships. System 2 is comprised of the world view which relates to the dominant and orienting values, both spiritual and material. System 3 is comprised of the world of action which relates to how people are motivated and make decisions. System 4 is comprised of the individual and world which relates the primary sources of identity, the demands of individualism and the requisites of the group (Wright, 1983, pp. 16-19).

Another paradigm for understanding the frame of reference of an ethnic minority family are the constructs of help seeking behavior and the ethnographic interview (Green, 1982). Green has proposed a model for understanding how an ethnic minority family defines a problem. The model seeks to examine the help seeking behavior of the family in order to gain insight into how the family perceives a problem. In order to understand the cultural characteristics of the family, one must begin with the language and labels the family uses to explain what is being experienced. In addition, it is important to recognize that the experience of a problem is both a personal and social event. It is personal since it produces individual discomfort. It is social in that the perception of the experience often requires confirmation of others before corrective action can be taken. Green's framework has four major components:

"1.   The client's recognition of an experience as a problem.

2.   The client's use of language to label and categorize a problem.

3.   The availability of indigenous helping resources in client communities and the decision-making involved in the utilization of those resources.

4.   Client oriented criteria for determining that a satisfactory resolution has been achieved" (Green, 1982, p. 31).

Another technique to understand a family's frame of reference is the ethnographic interview (Green, 1982). The ethnographic interview is proposed as a technique to move beyond the culturally bound approaches in information gathering with ethnic and minority clients. Such an interview should be thought of as a friendly conversation in which the interviewer clarifies the purpose of the conversation and then offers procedural explanations during the interview. Green suggests that in some respects the family must be viewed as an expert in defining their problem and the family's opinions must be clearly understood before analysis of the problem can begin. The process is to be straight forward and the worker should avoid deep interpretations about the "true nature" of the problem. Green identifies three prescriptions for the ethnographic interview. First, the interviewee plays the teaching role, and the interviewer acts as the student. Next, the interview is controlled by the interviewer, but through use of ethnographic material provided by the client. Third, the client's meaning of the information always acts as the central purpose of the interviewing (Green, 1982, p. 79).

Trust

Another important component of engaging low income African-American families in treatment is gaining each family member's trust. Boyd-Franklin (1990) supports this assertion indicating that gaining trust is important to beginning the

87

therapy process. If family workers strive toward creativity, there are numerous options for gaining family trust, and thus, beginning the engagement process with the family. One way to begin to build a trusting relationship with a family is to demonstrate one's current cultural awareness and willingness to learn from the families themselves.

Another method for developing trust which is derived from Structural Family Therapy is joining (Boyd-Franklin, 1990; Raider, 1989). The method of joining was originally developed by Salvidor Minuchin in 1974. Family workers may find Minuchin's technique of adapting to the family's affective style to be useful in work with low-income, urban, African-American families. To do this, one immediately learns the family's language patterns and commonly used terms. Minuchin shares anecdotes about himself as he feels that these relate to the family discussion. He describes this therapeutic style as acting like a distant relative, joining a family system and accommodating to its style (Minuchin, 1974). Considering the African American value of extended family, acting like a distant relative may prove quite consistent with this cultural component. Joining serves the purpose of letting the family know that the therapist is working for them and with them (Goldenberg & Goldenberg, 1991). For these families who have often found that social service agencies worked against them, such a technique may prove immensely useful.

In his work with religious families, Raider described joining as a means of relating personally, yet professionally, with families for therapeutic purposes. Raider has identified methods used in the joining process which may be used to engage low-income, urban, African-American families. In the joining process, Raider identifies the methods of *professional self-disclosure, tracking* and *accommodation* (Raider, 1989). These approaches have often been used to engage ethnic minority families.

Professional Self-Disclosure

Professional self-disclosure seems to be effective in counseling low-income, urban, African-American families since this method does not involve a direct immediate focus on what is wrong with the family. Since many African-American families have had the negative experience of being blamed for their problems, an immediate focus on existing problems may discourage some of these families from staying in treatment.

The importance of self-disclosure derives from Lum's view regarding the importance of professional self-disclosure whereby a point of interest common to the client and the worker becomes a means of forming a relationship. Lum's position is based on the belief that ethnic and minority clients approach human service agencies with reservations about professional helpers. Lum offers the following practical suggestions:

"Introduce yourself, share pertinent background about your work, family and helping philosophy. Find a point of common interest with the client. Revealing oneself as a human being affords the client an opportunity to assess character and form a tentative impression of the worker." (Lum, 1986, p. 104).

There are many conceptualizations of self-disclosure. McCarthy (1978) and Nilsson (1979) defined two different types of therapists' self-disclosure. First, were responses or statements referring to the past history or personal experiences of the therapist outside the therapy session. These were called self-disclosing statements by McCarthy (1978) and interpersonal statements by Nilsson (1979). Second, were responses that were direct expressions of the therapists' present feelings about or reactions to the statements and/or behaviors of the client. These were called self-involving statements by McCarthy (1978) and intrapersonal statements by Nilsson (1979).

Hoffman-Graff (1977) also identified self-disclosing statements into two types; first, there was positive self-disclosure, which involved interviewer

89

statements that revealed positive strengths, positive experiences and/or personal characteristics and second, there was negative self-disclosure, which involved interviewer statements that revealed personal foibles, negative experiences and/or personal characteristics.

In addition to forms of self-disclosure specified above, it seems that therapists and family workers disclose much about themselves during sessions, nonverbally through body language, dress, and appearance; and by verbally expressing attitudes, preferences and opinions. A useful approach to practicing self-disclosure with low income African-American families is to utilize a point of common interest which becomes a means of forming a relationship. Revealing oneself as a human being enables families to form a tentative impression of the therapist.

Accommodation and Tracking

Accommodation involves the worker's acceptance of the family's customs and practices, thereby showing respect for the family's communication channels, rules, norms, religion, culture, race, ethnicity and frame of reference (Raider, 1989). Similar to this method, *tracking,* occurs as family workers adopt symbols of the family's life which may be gathered from observing and listening to communication between family members. These symbols may include life themes, values and family events (Goldenberg & Goldenberg, 1991; Minuchin, 1974; Raider, 1989), and may be used by the family worker in conversation with the family as he/she gradually comes to understand the meaning of their significance. Through this type of conversation, the family worker confirms that what family members have to say is valuable, though, without directly soliciting information from the family. This method also influences later transactional patterns (Goldenberg & Goldenberg, 1991). Minuchin refers to this as "leading by following" (Minuchin, 1974). *Tracking* a certain family theme may also provide clues to the family structure (Goldenberg & Goldenberg, 1991).

Hines and Boyd-Franklin (1982) have asserted that African-American

90

females are more likely than their male partners to initiate or be open to family therapy as a means of working through relationship problems. Family workers may have to make special efforts to engage African-American males in family therapy. Even if there is limited involvement of a father (or mother), therapists may use phone contacts or letters to keep that parent abreast of the family's treatment progress (Hines & Boyd-Franklin, 1982).

Case Illustration

Strategy: Show understanding of the family's cultural frame of reference in order to engage them in the treatment process. Develop trust through use of tracking, accommodation, and professional self-disclosure.

The Pryer family was successfully engaged in home-based family counseling through crisis intervention. In addition to family counseling, the family also began receiving case management services. As a result of effective crisis intervention, the family began working with Ms. Venton, a home-based family social worker and Mr. Trith, a case manager at Ryan Behavioral Health Services. The family had received previous services from several workers at Ryan Behavioral Health Services and they participated in various programs at the agency. However, each time services were discontinued due to Mrs. Pryer's withdrawal or a social worker's discharge due to inconsistency with appointments. After assisting Mrs. Pryer by providing crisis intervention initially, both Mr. Trith and Ms. Venton introduced themselves to Mrs. Pryer and the family by disclosing information about their professional backgrounds. This technique helped to build rapport with the family. When Mr. Trith mentioned that he had previously worked at a youth recreation program, 12 year-old, Evan (one of the children in the family) became alert, and stated, "Oh yeah, I've been there. That's a cool place."

Ms. Venton and Mr. Trith successfully accomplished an initial engagement, but their next challenge was to work to keep the family engaged long enough to accomplish service goals. Mrs. Pryer, age 27, was separated from her husband of 10 years and currently caring for her 7 children alone. Mrs. Pryer's children ranged in age from 14 to 1 year old: Marx, 14; Evan, 12; Lila, 10; Mila, 9; Kesia, 7; Fresia, 4; and Aron, 1. The Pryers had moved four times since their first contact with the agency; and their phone number was often disconnected or changed. The social workers at this agency knew that this family was in need of help, but staying connected with them was often a problem. At the time of the initial engagement, Mrs. Pryer frantically reported that Evan had been kicked out of school for fighting, and Evan's teacher and principal told her that he would not be allowed to continue at school until he received counseling. At the time of this crisis Mrs. Pryer was angry with the school system as she stated that the school principal threatened to call Protective Services on her because she was late in picking Evan up from school that day. Mrs. Pryer stated that she was tired of everyone blaming her; and that "if the social workers at Ryan Behavioral Health Services had done their jobs properly in the past, the problem would not have come to this." Ms. Venton's and Mr. Troth's immediate response to this crisis was their first step toward successful engagement.

As they worked to further engage the Pryer family in counseling, Ms. Venton and Mr. Trith worked to understand the family's ethnic frame of reference. During an early session, Ms. Venton asked each family member (except for Aron) to name one family problem. This helped Ms. Venton to get to know the family. It also helped each family member to understand that his / her input was important. Ms. Venton paid a great deal of attention to what Mrs. Pryer thought the family problems were. To give Mrs. Pryer control of the session, she asked Mrs. Pryer which of the family problems mentioned (by herself and the other family members) were the most important to work on. Although family counseling would be geared toward helping all family members, the current focus would be on Mrs. Pryer and Evan. It was Ms. Venton's belief that if one helps the mother, one also helps the children. Before beginning the session, Ms. Venton reminded herself that gaining trust would be important to the engagement process. Mrs. Pryer had previously stated that she felt betrayed. Mrs. Pryer had difficult experiences with the social service system and thus, gaining trust would present a challenge to Ms. Venton and Mr. Trith. During this following early session, Ms. Venton gave Mrs. Pryer much of the control over the counseling process.

Ms. Venton: Out of everything that the children and you have said, Mrs. Pryer, can you choose two or three things that are you think are most important to focus on right now?

Mrs. Pryer: Two or three things, Gosh, all of what they said was true and good, I don't know where to start. There are so many things. I get so confused sometimes. I feel like I have all these people telling me what to do, and I can't always do all of these things by myself.

Ms. Venton: Yes, when you think of things that you want to work on it can be overwhelming and confusing.

Mrs. Pryer : I guess Evan has a lot of problems at school right now. Even though I'm kind of glad we're separated and my husband, Buddy is out of the house, I still have a hard time without him. I don't know where he is right now, so I can't call him if I need help with the kids, and I know that the kids miss him. We haven't heard from him for months. Buddy's taken off before, but we've never been away from him for this long.

Ms. Venton: Would it be a good idea to begin services by opening cases for you and Evan, and providing family sessions when they're needed.

Mrs. Pryer: That would be good, but will we still get to have family therapy with all of us present?

Ms. Venton: Yes, Mr. Trith and I would like to work with your whole family, and everyone is welcome to participate, but we would like two of you to help us develop service plans in order to begin the process. The purpose of the service plans will be to ensure that we are helping to work on things that are important to you.

93

Mrs. Pryer: So Evan and I will get to choose our own goals?

Ms. Venton: Yes, and you will be able to do the same thing when Mr. Trith comes over a little later. We won't end our session today until you are satisfied with the goals and objectives you have chosen.

Mrs. Pryer: What are objectives?

Ms. Venton: Those are "baby-steps" toward your goals. In other words, those are things that you do to help you to reach your goals. If you can chose one thing that you want to work on, I can show you how it works.

Mrs. Pryer: O.K. , let's see... I want to feel like I'm a good mother. I feel so down sometimes. I don't have too many friends because I've had some bad experiences, and I don't trust anyone; and a lot of my family members are dead, so I don't have much family support. I don't drive because I don't have my license, so I feel alone a lot of the time. Some nights, I stay awake and worry about how I can do all these things for my kids all by myself. I get to where I start feeling helpless and hopeless.

Ms. Venton: It sounds like a lot of people have let you down in your life, so you don't trust people; and yet you need help from people so that you and your children can survive and be happy.

Mrs. Pryer: Yeah, and when all a lot of times I do ask people for help and they actually help me it turns out to be a disaster. Like the time I had a neighbor lady watch the kids and she robbed us. We are still afraid of her. That's part of the reason why we moved. And then there's my "ex" or almost "ex". He hasn't done anything to help us.

Ms. Venton: You guys have had a lot of disappointments. How are all of you dealing with this?

Mrs. Pryer: Well, I just try to take things one day at a time. Going to Church was good for us, but we haven't been to our old Church since we moved. I also felt like a lot people passed judgement on me after I separated from Buddy, so I wasn't too comfortable there anyway.

94

Ms. Venton: A lot of times Churches are good sources of support, especially when people are going through difficult times. I know that my own church has begun to offer recreational activities and various types of support groups and people have really taken advantage of them.

Mrs. Pryer: What kind of Church do you go to?

Ms. Venton: It's a non-denominational Church that I have been going to for about the past five years.

Mrs. Pryer: I have thought about checking out a non-denominational church that is close to here. We used to go to a Baptist Church. Buddy was really into it, and in some ways, I was too; but I wouldn't mind looking into other Churches, maybe a non-denominational Church.

Ms. Venton: Would you like Mr. Trith and I to help you locate a nearby Church?

Mrs. Pryer: Sure, that would help us. We need all the support we can get right now.

Ms. Venton: You and your family have really been through a lot. All of you are survivors. What else helped you to get through these difficult times?

Mrs. Pryer: Well, it used to help me to have family meetings; but lately, things have been in such a mess, we haven't had one in a while. The other thing is that the kids get really wild lately, and I can't seem to control them enough so that we can have a meeting that actually makes sense.

Ms. Venton: Well, if family meetings have helped you before, do you think that I could help you run a family meeting and we could include these as part of your service plan.

Mrs. Pryer: That might be good.

Ms. Venton: You have some good ideas, Mrs. Pryer. Based on all that we've talked about so far what would you like to work on for yourself?

Mrs. Pryer: Oh, yeah, my goals. Let's see… I would like to be able to have a friend or two who I can trust; and I would like to find ways to help me and the kids to adjust to the bad things that have happened to us.

95

Ms. Venton: That sounds like a great place to start.

Case Illustration Discussion

As one can see, the Pryer family faced many social, economic and political struggles. In fact, part of Mrs. Pryer's confusion seemed to come from the various political systems which became involved in her life. These systems include the school, mental health and social service systems. Ms. Venton's awareness of Mrs. Pryer's mistrust of social agencies was helpful to the further engagement which took place. Having a great deal of cultural awareness, Ms. Venton knew that this type of mistrust was typical for many African American families. Such mistrust seems to stem from the fact that social and counseling services were not always available to African Americans. Not having these services available to them, African Americans have been inclined to think that these types of services are only for those who are white and wealthy. Although this perception may be considered healthy paranoia, it presents obvious challenges to the effective engagement of African American families in counseling. In addition to having this natural mistrust of social agencies, Mrs. Pryer's mistrust was compounded by her difficult life experiences. Another barrier to the effective engagement process was Ms. Venton's ethnicity. Ms. Venton, a white social worker, anticipated some feelings of mistrust coming from Mrs. Pryer; but her cultural awareness and her ability to engage Mrs. Pryer in a conversation rather than having a didactic session in which she told Mrs. Pryer what to do was a helpful step toward overcoming this barrier. It is also important to remember that it was not only white people who Mrs. Pryer did not trust, she really did not trust anyone. In addition , it is possible that if Ms. Venton had been an African American female therapist, Mrs. Pryer could have viewed her as a traitor.

As part of building rapport in her relationship with Mrs. Pryer, Ms. Venton explored the family's frame of reference. In this exploration, Ms. Venton asked questions geared toward gaining information about each family's member's understanding of the family problems. Her conversation with Mrs. Pryer focused on Mrs. Pryer's identification of the problems which she felt were significant. This method differs from various traditional methods in which the therapist identifies the problem and then tells the consumer what he / she should be doing to solve the problem. In the course of the conversation, Mrs. Pryer alluded that this type of "intervention" was frustrating to her when she stated. " There are so many things. I get so confused sometimes. I feel like I have so many people telling me what to do, and I can't do all of these things by myself". This statement also seems to reveal that Mrs. Pryer was tired and frustrated by social service agencies that placed many demands on her without providing the resources and help she needed to meet these demands. In her own way, she could have been asking Ms. Venton if she too would make such demands on her. Therefore, Ms. Venton's choice to let Mrs. Pryer take control of problem identification was wise.

As Mrs. Pryer identified family problems, Ms. Venton asked about the family's coping mechanisms. Mrs. Pryer's explanations would be helpful resources in helping the family reach their goals. This was a form of *accommodation* in which Ms. Venton was attempting to become familiar rules and norms in the Pryer family. The Church involvement and family meetings were signs that the family had coping skills which they could use. During this time of difficult adjustment, Ms. Venton and Mr. Trith would work with the family in order to strengthen their current coping skills. Since Mrs. Pryer had negative experiences with social agencies, there would be a chance that she would follow the pattern of discontinuing services due to mistrust. Thus, it would be essential to work toward the development of a trusting relationship with Mrs. Pryer and her family. During this session, Ms. Venton used the service plan to develop a mutual contract between herself and Mrs. Pryer. This mutual contract could be used to begin a relationship based on mutual respect so that Mrs. Pryer could perceive Ms. Venton and Mr. Trith as her peers rather than authority figures.

Ms. Venton had already begun to use *tracking* by gathering information about the family's values and events. Mrs. Pryer seemed to place value on Church support; and a significant family event was Mr. Pryer's leaving the famlily. At the end of the session, Ms. Venton showed interest in being a part of one of the family meetings mentioned by Mrs. Pryer. During this time, Ms. Venton would observe communication between family members, as she would further use the *tracking* technique.

Family Assessment:

In carrying out family assessments Boyd-Franklin (1990) stresses that therapists must remember to ask the right questions. This means that one must use knowledge of African-American culture when asking questions of family members. For low-income, urban, African-Americans, questions related to the five framework components are extremely important. It is also important to ask appropriate questions before making potentially erroneous assumptions. For example, one should not assume that all of the members that are present in the first family meeting are biological relatives. Boyd-Franklin (1990) shares the African-American aphorism that "It takes a whole tribe to raise a child." This maxim reflects the extended family dynamics which are seen in cases of multiple mothering and informal adoption (Boyd-Franklin, 1990). Mothers living in female-headed households may be given child care support from others in their extended families. It is important to be aware that these family members may be called "mother", "cousin" or "aunt" as a form of respect although they are not biologically related to the children. Another example involves religion and spirituality. Boyd-Franklin (1990) states that for most African-Americans, spirituality is inherent and intrinsic; and Beverly (1995) asserts that any psychosocial assessment of African-Americans should extend to include the spiritual domain. Relevant questions that a worker might ask in regard to spirituality are: "What do you do when there isn't anything else to do?;" or "Given everything that has happened to you, how do you find the strength to keep going?"

(Beverly, 1995, p. 19)

One of the best ways to assess the entire African-American family is by going on home visits. This is also the most effective way to meet the most powerful and influential family members, since the least powerful family members may be those most likely to come into family therapy (Boyd-Franklin, 1990). Often, the most powerful and influential family members may include grandmothers, aunts, fathers, boyfriends, and cousins (1990). It is also important for the family therapist assessing low-income, urban, African-American families to identify family strengths, which are not always evident when families first initiate treatment. For this reason, it is important that family workers strive to develop present and potential strengths. As previously mentioned, families may have greater comfort with this method of assessment rather than a method in which the worker focuses immediately and only on the family problems.

Although building family strengths is important, families who enter into family counseling do so because they are dealing with problems. Due to these problems, family strengths which are present may not be readily apparent. Thus, skillful integration in which both problems as well as these family strengths which will be used to overcome problems is necessary. This approach may be found in many family preservation programs, which aim to keep children at home with their families. Such programs seem to have been successful both in acknowledging strengths while at the same time showing awareness of family problems (Kinney, Haapala, & Booth, 1991). Both of these strategies are essential and complementary to assessment and services provided to low-income, urban, African-American families. Here, the Homebuilders model assessment guidelines which have been previously discussed in regard to the strength / resilience framework component are useful strategies. For example, the guidelines used in the Homebuilder model include use of problem definitions as constructs rather than perceptions of reality; recognition of unique challenges presented by families in crises, and the vulnerability which may surface during these times; and use of assessments which focus on both family strengths and problems (Kinney, Haapala, & Booth, 1991).

Just as workers strive to gain the family's trust, workers must also learn to trust the family. One basic way of doing this is for workers to trust that the family members have the best data about their situation. At times, family workers may rush to check information from past professional reports. Such reports may be limited if previous workers were not able to spend a great deal of time with the family of if the workers did not have the opportunity to view family members in their natural environments (Kinney, Haapala, & Booth, 1991).

The initial assessment phase lays the groundwork needed for generating options for change. In work with low-income, urban, African-American families, workers need to show awareness of problems which occur at many different levels: the home, neighborhood, school, the religious community, social agencies and so on. In this way, an ecological perspective is utilized. This perspective acknowledges the influence of the environment on human and family functioning and encourages workers to examine the context in which individuals develop. Thus, the worker considers individuals who interact with family, friends, co-workers, the religious community, cultural and socioeconomic factors. From the ecological perspective, individuals have potential both for developmental growth and developmental derailment depending on environmental supports and risks, and other characteristics, as well as their own inherent qualities (Whitelaw-Downs, 1994).

Case Illustration

During the assessment and service planning process, acknowledge family strengths as well as problems.

Curtis Rones, age 12, had been referred to a children's home-based community mental health program after being hospitalized twice in an inpatient setting; participation in a partial-day counseling program and an outpatient

100

program. Curtis was diagnosed with Conduct Disorder (First, 1994) and he also had a learning disability and a deformity on his hand. The primary presenting problem was that Curtis acted out aggressively at home and at school and often destroyed property. Curtis lived at home with his mother, Rita Rones; father, Herman Rones and 17-year-old brother, Sherman Rones. At the time of the last hospitalization, Mrs. Rones stated that she was "ready to give up and put Curtis in a boys' home." However, the child and family outpatient worker who had begun work with Curtis and his family offered other options to Mrs. Rones in this time of crisis. The following dialogue demonstrates how the child and family outpatient therapist, Mr. Jackson, focused on the family's strengths in order to help them to find a program which was better suited to their needs at this time.

Mrs. Rones: I'll tell you, Mr. Jackson, I don't think that I can take this anymore. We're hospitalizing Curtis today, and if things don't get better after that, I think I'll just send him to a boys' home. It's best for our family. We cannot let Curtis break our phone, threaten us and hit us. I'm worried that one of us is going to get hurt. My husband, and Sherman have held their temper with Curtis, but they can only take so much before they will lash out at Curtis.

Mr. Jackson: Your family has struggled with Curtis' difficult behaviors because all of you love and care about him so much. Sending Curtis to any kind of a residential program or boys' home would be hard on all of you. Before, you do something like that, I would like to tell you about another alternative. Our agency has a program for youth who have been hospitalized or in other out-of -home placements at least twice. The purpose of this home-based program is to keep the children at home with their families and to prevent further hospitalizations or out-of-home placements. The counseling that is done is quite intense, and the therapist must meet with you at least two times weekly. All of the counseling takes place at the client's home.

Mrs. Rones: Well, that might work. At this point, I'm willing to try anything. I'm certainly not happy that Curtis has to go to the hospital again; and since part of the problem with outpatient services was that Curtis often refused to come, this might be better. My worry is that if Curtis finds out that a therapist is coming to the house, he might leave.

Mr. Jackson: We can explain to Curtis how much all of you want him to stay at home with you, and maybe that will help. You may also want to tell him about the other alternative that you were considering.

Mrs. Rones: Yeah, I guess that no matter what problems he has he has to either deal with them or face the consequences.

Mr. Jackson: You are a very concerned and patient mother, Mrs. Rones. So far, you have tried many different ways to help Curtis; and now I' m offering one more.

Mrs. Rones: I have tried a lot of things and I guess that trying one more way to help him can't hurt. After all, we have to do something.

Mr. Jackson kept in touch with Curtis and his family during the hospitalization by phone; and by attending team meetings held at the hospital. He also met with Curtis while Curtis was in the hospital. During this meeting, Curtis was very angry, and he threatened Mr. Jackson. Even at this time, Mr. Jackson attempted to build on whatever strengths were present in order to diffuse the situation.

Mr. Jackson: Hi, Curtis, how are you doing?

Curtis: Why are you here? I hate you. You're the one who put me here and now you ask how I'm doing!

Mr. Jackson: You don't like it here, Curtis?

Curtis: No, I hate here and I'd like to break you in half for sending me here.

Mr. Jackson: Well, where would you rather be?

Curtis: Out. On the streets. With my friends, anywhere except here.

Mr. Jackson: Tell me about your friends, Curtis.

Curtis: No.

(There was a two minute silence as Curtis refused to talk and he began banging his fist against the wall.)

Mr. Jackson: Do you think that acting like this is going to get you out of here. Do you think that this kind of behavior will help you get your way?

(Curtis stopped banging his fist against the wall and sat down across from Mr. Jackson.)

Mr. Jackson: Thanks for not breaking me in half and thanks for bringing your temper under control event though you're really angry.

Curtis: They don't let me see anyone in here. My friends are mostly my cousins, and I can't even see them. My mom is talking about putting me away forever, and then I'll never be able to go out or see anyone.

Mr. Jackson: Your mom wants to keep you safe. She has considered placing you in a residential program because she is afraid that you will hurt someone or someone will hurt you if you continue to stay at home. Where you go after this hospitalization depends on your behavior.

Curtis: I guess I want to go home. I do miss everybody.

Mr. Jackson: I told your mother about a home-based counseling program that you could participate in. That means that your therapist would meet with you at least twice per week and your counseling is done at home with you and your family.

Curtis: Better than getting locked up, I guess.

Case Illustration Discussion

As Mr. Jackson wrote his progress note for this meeting with Curtis, he was able to identify strengths, and areas in which Curtis had made progress. The problems seemed obvious; and in many ways, acknowledging the problems present helped Mr. Jackson to identify strengths. Mr. Jackson thought about Curtis' anger about being placed in the hospital. To some extent, this seemed to be a healthy reaction. It meant that Curtis wanted to go back home. In fact, Curtis did state that he missed "everybody". Although Curtis had an anger outburst, he was able to calm down and begin talking to Mr. Jackson again. Mr. Jackson considered this an area of progress since Curtis had walked out of other sessions when he became angry. Mr. Jackson also thought that Curtis seemed afraid of "being locked up". This was also a healthy reaction.

Curtis and his family chose to participate in the home-based program. Mr. Jackson talked with the home-based therapist, Mr. Ford, who would work with the family. Mr. Jackson described the family as having a great deal of loyalty. He told Mr. Ford that Curtis' parents were very committed to helping Curtis and they tried several methods and programs. At the last team meeting, just prior to discharge, Mr. Jackson brought the new home-based therapist who would be working with Curtis and his family. During this time, the team of professionals, Curtis, and his family helped Mr. Ford to get to build a new home-based service plan which was strength-focused.

The strengths identified included Curtis' success in meeting the goals specified on his hospital service plan; his motivation to return home; his parents' commitment to having Curtis stay at home; family loyalty; Curtis' progress in his anger management; the healthy anger expressed at being separated from family and friends; the family's genuine concern for Curtis. In further developing the service plan, these strengths could be used as "weapons" to attack the problems which would also be identified. The primary problem identified was: Daily anger outbursts sometimes accompanied by physical aggression which presents a risk to self and others. (This type of physical aggression includes destruction of property and physical fighting). The goal related to this problem was : Consumer will use positive anger management skills to deal with anger. Objectives (steps toward this goal) included: Consumer will identify the source of his anger and share this information with family members; and Consumer and family members will brainstorm a list of anger management techniques; and Consumer and a family member will report successful use of at least one anger management technique each week for 5 consecutive weeks.

As Mr. Ford worked with Curtis and his family, he began to build on the family's supportive attitude and Curtis' motivation to stay at home. When Curtis was able to say that he was often angry because people made fun of him at school because of his learning disability and his deformed hand, all family members were supportive. Mr. Ford explained that this sounded like a case of displaced anger since Curtis often took much of his anger out on family members rather than the bullies at school. Another session focused on helping Curtis to find ways to deal with his anger as Curtis and his family brainstormed about anger management techniques. Curtis' brother stated that he used playing basketball as an outlet for his anger. Curtis liked the idea of using sports as an outlet for anger. On week nights, Curtis began to play a fifteen minute game of basketball with his brother. For his thirteenth birthday, the family bought Curtis a punching bag which he reported using often to "get things out of my system after a bad day."

Service Setting and Schedule

It is important to choose an appropriate setting in which the worker plans to engage families (Whitelaw-Downs, 1994; Wasik, Bryant & Lyons, 1990). When considering an effective social service setting in which to engage these families, one must show sensitivity and awareness as to where the families are and how to make services accessible to them. Engaging the families in settings in which they are comfortable and close-to-home is essential to the engagement process. If family workers are flexible and creative, options abound. However, therapists may need to extend themselves to engage these families in the therapeutic process (Hines & Boyd-Franklin, 1982). Often, these families may be most readily engaged if they are on their own turf. Programs which employ outreach strategies such as "neighborhood-based" family support services (Whitelaw-Downs, 1994), school-based family services (Raider & Steele, 1991), and home-based family services (Wasik, Bryant & Lyons, 1990) may be most relevant to the needs of low-income African-American families. The following program descriptions provide rationale for utilization of these programs:

- **Home-based services:** Based on home-visits, family-workers immediately conduct an informal assessment of the family's needs. These programs often apply a crisis intervention model as they assess family needs. An important guideline in home-based programs states that the family worker must first be responsive to the immediate needs of the family before working toward long-term goals. In work with low-income families, it is typical for workers to see that the family is in crisis due to the lack of some concrete need. For example, there may be a need to help the family provide healthy meals for its children or to obtain quality care for a sick family member. Through the assessment, the worker will decide whether to call for assistance from other professionals; or to simply assist the family members in meeting concrete needs through his /her own efforts (Wasik, Bryant & Lyons, 1990).

- **School-based Services:** In response to the needs of youth in urban environments, various mental health professionals have begun to collaborate with teachers, other school professionals and community, civic, and religious organizations to create school-based/school-linked programs. These programs are consistent with the issues involved in the provision of treatment to low-income urban African-American families. School-community collaboration stands in the forefront of innovative programs which aim to serve youth using prevention and support techniques (Franklin & Streeter, 1995; Armbruster, Gerstein, & Fallon, 1997; Flaherty, Weist, & Warner, 1996).

- **Community-based/Outreach Services:** Engaging low-income urban African-American families in settings which are comfortable and close to home proves to be essential to an engagement process in which family members begin to build a trusting relationship with the helping profession. Since low-income, urban, African-American families are most readily engaged on their own turf, community-based and outreach programs may be among those that are most effective in working with the target population. In these types of programs, workers are required to go where the families and children are rather than having the families and children come to them (Downs, 1994). Community-based/outreach programs provide workers with the basis to employ many creative engagement strategies. Even traditional outpatient services may be more effective if there is a high level of collaboration with community organizations, schools, church and case managers.

Case Illustration

Strategy : Choose a treatment setting and schedule which is conducive to the family's needs.

Mrs. Brickman was told by her Family Independence Agency (FIA) worker, Ms. Dixon, that she needed to get counseling for her six-year-old granddaughter, Mati. Mrs. Brickman had become responsible for taking care of Mati after her son, Brian was shot and killed in a drive-by shooting. (Brain was previously Mati's primary caregiver). After her father's death, Mati lived with her mother, Sherry, for a brief time, but she was taken from her mother due to neglect. Mati had just turned six when her father died, and she heard the gun shots since he was just outside the house. Mrs. Brickman, a 55 years-old grandmother, walked with a cane due to leg problems. At the time of her request for services, she was the primary caregiver for four of her grandchildren. Mrs. Brickman, Mati, and the family had been participating in outpatient therapy, but when the family car was stolen, Mrs. Brickman was unable to get to the clinic and her case was closed. Mrs. Brickman agreed with the Ms. Dixon that therapy for Mati was needed since she was having nightmares about her mother and father about five times per week. In addition, Mati's teacher, Mrs. Bloom, expressed concern because Mati seemed withdrawn. Mrs. Bloom reported that although Mati's Kindergarten records describe her as a happy child who was eager to learn, Mati's current behaviors in first grade included daydreaming and limited interaction with the other children in social, play, and academic activities. The outpatient clinic where Mrs. Brickman and the family used to go was often inconvenient because the therapy offices were on an upstairs level and Mrs. Brickman had trouble getting up the stairs with her cane. Thus, Mrs. Brickman's FIA worker suggested that Mati participate in a school-based mental health program located in Mati's school. Since this type of mental health service was new, Mrs. Brickman had questions about the program.

The following dialogue demonstrates how Ms. Dixon's knowledge of the program made Mrs. Brickman and Mati more comfortable with getting involved; and it shows how the school-based setting was conducive to the family's needs. (Mati was also present during this meeting).

Ms. Dixon: I know that things did not work out well for you in outpatient services, so I would like to tell you about another program that might work better for you. I recently found out that there is a school-based mental health program where Mati attends school. The program offers individual child and family therapy; and case management services.

Mrs. Brickman: You mean I would have to go to school for Mati's therapy sessions?

Ms. Dixon: That would be one option. However, therapists are able to do homevisits. For individual sessions, the therapist can meet with Mati during lunch hour, or free hour. The therapist can also meet with Mati if she has a difficult day. Sometimes this may prevent her from getting into trouble at school. Since the therapists work at the school, it is easy for them to do classroom observations, and to work closely with teachers to improve school behavior and academic progress. The therapist can also keep you informed about how Mati is doing in school.

Mrs. Brickman: Mrs. Bloom is already worried about Mati because she is withdrawn and doesn't participate a whole lot right now. Is it going to be a problem if Mati attends a counseling session during class time? I mean, will she have to miss more school, and will missing school time really be good for her? What if Mrs. Bloom counts it against her? It worries me because she has already fallen behind a little.

Mrs. Dixon: Your concern is a valid one. I agree that it is not a good idea for Mati to miss school. The therapists in the school-based program feel the same way. That's why they have worked things out with the teachers to make sure that counseling does not interfere with class time. The therapists have had to make their schedules very flexible. For example, if a student in the program finishes his or her schoolwork early, the student may simply ask the teacher for permission to see the counselor. Other sessions may occur during free/study periods or during lunch time. During the lunch sessions, the students eat with their counselor. There may even be times when a student is having behavioral problems and the student may need to meet with the counselor to help to resolve an immediate school conflict. . If a therapist is doing a classroom observation, the therapist may be instrumental in helping students and teachers to resolve a classroom conflict. This is also considered a session. Other sessions, such as home-visit sessions, may be held after school hours.

Mrs. Brickman: Will everybody in the school end up knowing about Mati's problems: the kids, the teacher, the principal... ?

Mrs. Dixon: That's a really good question, and it is something that school-based therapists are working on. They understand that privacy and confidentiality are important, but sometimes children and even teachers or other school professionals reveal information that should be kept private. To address this problem, the school-based mental health program at Mati's school is has a training program that all teachers and students attend regarding this issue. School-based therapists do not reveal the content of any session to anyone unless there is a specific issue that needs to be addressed with a school professional and even in these cases, only the information regarding the issue at hand is discussed.

Mrs. Brickman: That sounds reasonable. Does it cost any thing to be in the program?

Mrs. Dixon: No, the program is free and it is offered to any child in the school who may need counseling services.

Mrs. Brickman: How often do home-visits occur?

Mrs. Dixon: That needs to be discussed with you and a therapist, but typically home-visits occur about two times monthly. If you are able to come to the school, or you are coming to a school meeting appointments to meet in the office are also available.

Mrs. Brickman: Are the school therapists trained to deal with problems that are not typical "school problems"? For instance would they be able address the problems that Mati has with the nightmares and her parents' death?

Mrs. Dixon: Yes, these school-based therapists do not simply focus on school-related problems such as poor academics and disruptive classroom behavior, they have the same training as other clinical therapists, so they do the same types of counseling. The only difference in their location.

Mrs. Brickman: I think we'll give a try. If we don't like it, we can stop, right?

Mrs. Dixon: That's right. If you find that this program is not working out well for you, you always have the right to withdraw.

Mrs. Brickman: Based on everything that you've said, the program sounds like it would be pretty good if Mati will do it. Let's explain it to her and ask her.

(Mati is sitting on the floor comfortably playing with dolls).

Mrs. Brickman: Mati, would you like to talk with a counselor at school the same way that you talked with Ms. Woods (previous outpatient counselor)?

Mati: (Nods her head). O.K. Do I get time out of school to go see her?

Mrs. Dixon: Well, you will be able to see her at times like lunch hour or free hour or after school. At other times, your teacher and counselor will have to agree that

110

it is O.K. for you to leave class for counseling. We don't want you to miss important stuff at school, Mati.

Mati: Did you say that the counselor will come to my house the way that you do sometimes?

Mrs. Dixon: Yes, that's right. Sometimes, like when you don't have a ride to the school, the counselor will meet with you at home.

Mati: That will be fun. I can show the counselor my toys and play.

As the referral source, Mrs. Dixon played an active role in getting Mati and Mrs. Brickman started in the school-based mental health program. First, she called the program and she guided Mrs. Brickman through the screening process which involved a phone interview. The purpose of the phone interview was to gather general information so that an appointment for a face-to-face intake interview could be made. The therapist who conducted the screening interview offered the option of having a home-visit interview or an office interview at the school. Mrs. Dixon told Mrs. Brickman that she could transport her to the school-based office if she preferred to the office interview. Mrs. Brickman stated that this time she did prefer the office interview because she wanted to see where the school-based offices were located in the school; and she thought that she would be more comfortable getting to know the program this way. Thus, the screening therapist offered several appointment times for the intake interview, so it was easy for Mrs. Dixon and Mrs. Brickman to choose a time that worked for both of them. The screening therapist was also able to coordinate the appointment time with Mati's schedule so that she would not miss important parts of her school day.

Mrs. Dixon effectively implemented the process of linking Mrs. Brickman and Mati with services which fit well with their needs. She demonstrated knowledge of the school-based program and she was able to take time to answer Mrs. Brickman's questions. The intervention of providing flexibility and a treatment setting conducive to the family's needs really began with Mrs. Dixon.

111

She took time with Mrs. Brickman as she provided answers to Mrs. Brickman's questions about the school-based program. The information that she provided helped Mrs. Brickman and Mati to make a decision about whether the program might work for them.

Since Mrs. Brickman and Mati did not have transportation due to the loss of the family car, Mrs. Dixon offered to transport Mrs. Brickman to the intake interview. The school-based program offered home visits which would be useful to Mrs. Brickman and Mati at this time since their means of transportation was limited. The school-based program was also useful to Mati and Mrs. Brickman because of the problems that Mati was beginning to have at school.

As one might guess, Mrs. Dixon's referral to school-based services worked well for Mrs. Brickman and Mati. The therapist, Ms. Vermont, was able to observe Mati's withdrawn behavior in the classroom. She and Mati went out for lunch together. Mati enjoyed this and she really seemed to relax. Ms. Vermont asked Mati what kind of a day she was having, and she remarked that Mati looked sad this morning at school. Mati explained that she was thinking about her "poor mom and dad" and wondering if she would ever see them again. During another session, a home-visit, Mati further explained her sad feelings to Mrs. Brickman. Mrs. Brickman told Mati that her parents were now safe and in a happy place. Ms. Vermont initiated an activity in which Mrs. Brickman and Mati made a memory book filled with pictures of Mati's parents with Mati and other family members. They used family photos and some of the pictures were drawn by Mati.

Mrs. Vermont was able to see Mati in home, office, school and community settings (such as out at a restaurant for lunch). This was quite helpful as Ms. Vermont was able to make an assessment of each of these environments. Ms. Vermont was also able to gain a true picture of how Mati was coping in each of these environments. Such knowledge allowed her to provide services that applied to the family's needs. For example, during home visits, Ms. Vermont saw that although the house was orderly, it was in need of several repairs. Ms. Vermont also saw the family's need for dependable transportation. To address these concrete issues, Ms. Vermont linked the family with a school-based case manager who helped the Mrs. Brickman to locate lost-cost repair services and to budget the money needed to buy a new car. Having both the therapist and the case manger available to them was especially helpful to the Mrs. Brickman and Mati. When Ms. Vermont was not available there was a good chance that Mrs. Hook, the case manager would be.

The therapeutic settings in which Mrs. Brickman and Mati received services were easily accessible and comfortable. When she attended parent-teacher conferences, Mrs. Brickman would allow Mati to meet with Ms. Vermont and then stop by after the conferences to talk with Mati and Ms. Vermont together. Since the school-based office was located on the first floor, Mrs. Brickman no longer had to worry about trying to climb steps with her cane as she did in the child outpatient program.

Building on Family Strengths

Building on family strength throughout the treatment process allows family members to see their therapy as positive and will increase their motivation (Daly, Jennings, Beckett, & Leashore, 1995; McAdoo, 1995; Kaplan & Girard, 1994; Kinney, Haapala & Booth, 1991). Successful family workers are also likely to encourage all family members to participate actively in therapy. This way, family members do not feel that social services are something that is *happening to them* (Kaplan & Girard, 1994); rather, they feel that they are *making services happen.* Workers may promote active participation while also building trust by encouraging all family members to contribute their input to the development of the service plan, and the content of all family sessions (Kaplan & Girard, 1994). The trust and respect fostered by these techniques is essential to providing helpful services to low-income, urban, African-American families.

In therapy with low-income, urban, African-American families, workers must intervene at various levels, and positive relationships must be strived for during each intervention. Here, services which are systems-oriented combined with a strength perspective may prove useful. This type of approach would involve an assessment of family problems and strengths in relation to the family's structure, functioning and environmental context (McGoldrick, Preto, Hines, Moore & Lee, 1991).

Goal Setting

Low self-esteem, often fostered by racism for many African-American families (Wilson & Stith, 1991), may cause family members to expect to fail even at concrete tasks (Kaplan & Girard, 1994). Therefore, small tasks should be approached first to ensure success. When the goals are modest, tasks are made more manageable and this creates an environment where success is fostered, which in turn, lessens the likelihood of families once again being faced with failure. No matter how small each success may be, the greater the number of triumphs, the greater the elevation of the client's self-esteem. As confidence develops, the belief in the family's ability to problem-solve grows as well. Repeated success will promote and increase consumers' hope and confidence in themselves, and will therefore instill in them the belief that their situation can change. Goals should also be both observable and measurable. This is achieved by working with the family to identify specific measurable indicators of attainment of the goal (Raider, 1987). For example, the goal of "Improve relationship between mother and daughter" is broad and difficult to observe and measure. However, an indicator of improved relationship might be the decreased number of arguments per week between mother and daughter. A measurable indicator might be to reduce the number of arguments from 7 per week to 3 per week by the end of the month. Goals related feelings such as "To increase daughter's positive regard of mother" may be measured by using the process of scaling. This may be accomplished by assigning a point on a scale to daughter's present level of positive regard for mother and choosing a higher level on the scale which represents increased positive regard. For example, if daughter perceives her current level of positive

114

regard of mother is 2 on a 10 point scale, the goal might be to increase her level of positive regard to 6 on the scale by the end of six sessions. The use of observable and measurable indicators of desired behavioral and emotional change will enable families to monitor the progress they are making and may motivate them and commit them more to the treatment process. It may also ameliorate negative perceptions of therapy often held by low-income, urban, African-American families.

A goal-setting method used by the authors seems to accomplish the task of putting parents in charge while also empowering the entire family. This method, developed by Cloe Madanes & Jay Haley (1977) is derived from Strategic Family Therapy. The worker asks the family members to talk to each other to determine the nature of the problem and of the change that they desire. In most cases, the family comes up with one or more problems or changes. As the worker accepts these, family members become more motivated for change since the problems and changes identified are their own (Raider, 1989). Often low-income, urban African-American families may not enter therapy until problems are quite overwhelming and seemingly out of control (Boyd-Franklin, 1990). Consequently, it may be necessary to redefine overwhelming problems so that there are several smaller more manageable problems (Raider, 1989).

At this point, the worker may assist family members in identifying small changes that they would like to occur. At times, family members expect big changes immediately. Making the steps toward small improvement will help families to be realistic about goals rather setting themselves up to fail. Workers may also encourage individuals to select one or two goals while reminding them that change will occur gradually rather than all at once (Kinney, Haapla, & Booth, 1991).

Concrete Needs

In work with low-income urban African-American families, it may seem obvious that addressing the concrete needs of the family is of paramount importance. In work with high-risk families such as the identified population, Kaplan and Girard (1994) assert that professionals must respond to the families' immediate concrete needs. It may be helpful to clarify that concrete needs encompass a range of services which are directly related to the families' basic needs. Such services may include helping a family to secure housing, providing transportation, finding day care options, or assisting the family in developing a budget (Kaplan & Girard, 1994).

Earlier research is consistent with the stated importance of concrete social services. To work effectively with low-income, urban African-American families, workers must be able to expand the context and role of the therapy which they provide. As service providers, workers must be open to exploring the influence of social, political, socioeconomic, and other broad environmental factors with the families they serve. This concept has been identified as central to providing social services African-American inner-city families (McGoldrick, Pearce, Giordano, 1982).

It should be noted that low-income urban African-American families often feel overwhelmed with economic issues. These families may be faced with threatened eviction from their homes or termination of welfare payments. Survival issues such as these most often take precedence over family and psychological conflicts (McGoldrick, Pearce, Giordano, 1982). Keeping this in mind, workers may view concrete services as a means of building rapport and trust with the families. In this way providing concrete needs may be viewed as essential to effecting change, since this service offers a unique opportunity to establish a trusting partnership before psychological needs are addressed (Kaplan & Girard, 1994). When providing concrete services, it is not suggested that social workers and therapists assume familial responsibility; but rather, they should work to assist the families in using resources and contacts to meet their needs, and thus, to assist in facilitating change (Foley, 1975). In order to do this, workers must demonstrate willingness to do outreach work, and to expend the needed time and energy

116

(McGoldrick, Pearce, & Giordano, 1982).

Although there are few studies which specifically examine the effects of providing concrete services within a family-based context (Fraser, Pecora & Haapala 1991), there is evidence to support the positive effects of offering concrete services to families. For example, transportation, employment, and house-cleaning, represent types of child welfare services which have been recognized as ancillary to support working effectively with multiproblem families (Kaplan, 1986; Levine, 1964; Lewis, 1991). Bryce (1982, as cited in Frankel, 1988, p. 150) found that clients rated providing practical help such as concrete services; services in the home; and therapist availability and flexibility of hours as more helpful than specific therapeutic techniques. The Parents and Children Together (PACT) program also identified the provision of concrete services as vital to successful treatment (Van Meter, 1986).

Haapala's study (1983) has been one of few to test whether the provision of concrete services was significantly associated with treatment success. In this study, Haapala identified critical incidents which occurred in 41 single-parent families. Weekly, mothers, children, and therapists were asked to identify and rate events that took place during targeted sessions involving the therapist and one or more family member. Using qualitative methods, the events were categorized and then coded for statistical analysis. A discriminant analysis of the mothers' and children's data sets suggested that when the *Homebuilders* therapist supported the client in obtaining concrete services or such services were provided, treatment success was more likely to occur. In addition, the greater the number of times the therapist did something to encourage a family member to obtain some type of tangible service for the family or for a child in the family, the more likely the child was to remain at home as opposed to alternative placement (Haapala, 1983). Haapala proposed that providing hard services to families was certainly helpful in a tangible way. In addition, the message that what was most important to the client was also something that the worker perceived as the highest priority had powerful

117

meaning to the client.

Based on the information which supports the positive effects of providing concrete services, it is not surprising that families often identify immediate response to concrete needs as the most important service they have been provided (Fraser & Haapala, 1987-1988; Morton & Grigsby, 1993). Families' positive response to this initial help may be explained by three factors: Families, especially African-American families, may distrust social workers and therapists based on past experiences. Families may not respond well to "talk therapy"; and for many families, concrete assistance is needed in tasks such as completing applications and negotiating social service bureaucracies (Kaplan & Girard, 1994). As stated earlier, concrete needs must be met before families become motivated to address psychological needs. This is especially true for poor families. For example, a mother who is unable to make her food stamps last due to a lack of transportation is forced to pay higher prices at a store within walking distance and is so preoccupied with this basic human need that a note from her child's teacher stating that her child is not completing her homework may seem trivial in comparison. The mother in this situation, is worried that her child will not have enough food to eat; yet, part of the problem may be that the child is hungry and cannot concentrate on her homework in the evening. The simple solution of providing transportation to a supermarket would be a powerful intervention (Kaplan & Girard, 1994). Many African-American families may face situations such as the one previously described. For these families, dealing with concrete needs first may be less intimidating than initially addressing psychological issues. Families often see concrete needs as external, impersonal, separate from themselves, and less connected to their self-worth than emotional and psychological problems.

Problem-Solving Focus

Insight oriented psychotherapy which seeks to bring about change by helping the client to develop increased understanding of the origins of their maladaptive coping behaviors is often perceived by low-income African-American

118

families as impractical and irrelevant. Clients are likely to believe they are being blamed for their presenting problem. Therapy time spent exploring background events and experiences often appear as a waste of time in light of the urgency of the issues clients bring to the service provider.

A problem solving approach based upon behavioral, social learning and cognitive principles is likely to be perceived as more consistent with the experiences and world view of low-income African-American families. Such an approach (B.F. Skinner, 1953; Ullmann, L. & Krosner, L., 1965; Beck 1976) focuses on the problem at hand with emphasis on system relief or finding a solution to the problem confronting the family. The role of the family therapist or worker is authoritative rather than non-directive. The focus of work is behavior change. Emphasis is placed on the present rather than underlying motivations or rationales. In order to achieve change, families must be motivated to take action and it is the experience of new behavior which has been reinforced and/or generalized that produces change. Change also takes place through cognitive shifts which deactivate negative or maladaptive messages and interpretations of behaviors and events to a more neutral or positive message and interpretation . Although the change may be quite small, it may lead to much larger systemic change. The family and extended family system, however it may be configured, is the focus of change. Attention is shifted from the "identified client" to the family as a whole.

Case Illustration

Strategy: Utilize a problem solving approach.

Ms. Laper came to the Pine Valley Behavioral Health Center due to problems that she had been having with her twelve-year-old son, Casey. During her initial interview with her therapist Mrs. Mc Rand, Ms. Laper stated that Casey was "just hard-headed"; and she went on to explain that Casey just decided not to listen to anything that she said when he was not getting everything his way. As Mrs. Mc Rand began to work with Casey and his mother, she asked many questions about family relationships and Ms. Laper's discipline techniques with Casey and the other children. Mrs. Mc Rand thought that it might be helpful to have information about family history so that she could help Casey and his mother to understand the reasons behind Casey's behavior so that negative behaviors could be changed. During one particular session, both Ms. Laper and Casey became frustrated with these techniques, as demonstrated in the following dialogue.

Ms. Laper: Well, Mrs. Mc Rand, Casey is at it again. We have been evicted from our house, and my sister, Sylvia, is letting us stay at her place for a while, but Casey has decided to complain about it. He says he doesn't like it there. I told him that I just cannot find another place for him to stay right now. My sister is married and she has three children. It is a little crowded, but the rest of us are dealing with it. Just because he can't have his own way, he decides to make everyone in the house miserable. He bothers the other kids; he doesn't wake up for school on time; and he refuses to do chores. It is ridiculous. Now he says that he wants to run away.

(Mrs. Mc Rand turns to Casey.)

Mrs. Mc Rand: Why don't you like it there Casey?

Casey: I can't stand my uncle Roy. He's a total jerk. He tries to start fights with me.

Mrs. Mc Rand: Does fighting happen a lot in your family?

Casey: It happens sometimes.

Mrs. Mc Rand: Who usually does the fighting?

Casey: Well, everybody argues and fights at one time or another.

Mrs. Mc Rand: When did you start to think that your Uncle Roy was a jerk?

Casey: I don't really know. I just don't like him.

Mrs. Mc Rand: Are you angry with your mom for bringing you over to his house to live?

120

Casey: Sometimes.

Mrs. Mc Rand: Are you angry at your mom for any other reasons.

Casey: I'm mad when she makes me come here sometimes.

Ms. Laper: Look, Mrs. Mc Rand, I am tired of exploring reasons why Casey might be angry with me. I'm angry with him too, but right now we have to go. I have other children to pick up from school, and I have to get home and make dinner for my sister's children and my own. I promised to help my sister with certain things since I'm staying there.

Mrs. Mc Rand: Maybe if we can find out why Casey is acting this way, we can help him to change it.

Ms. Laper: Are you saying that I am the reason that he is acting this way?I'm tired of being called a bad parent. He teacher blames me; his father blames me and now I come here and you blame me. This just is not helping. I have too many other things to concentrate on.

Ms. Laper left the agency without scheduling another appointment. Mrs. Mc Rand thought about why Ms. Laper was frustrated with her. She recalled Ms. Laper's last statement: "I have too many other things to concentrate on." Ms. Laper also stated that she was tired of exploring reasons why Casey was angry with her. In addition, Ms. Laper's statements about others blaming her for Casey's behavior were important. Mrs. Mc Rand decided to look more closely at the current problem that was facing the family : their eviction from their home. Casey was probably not the only family member struggling with this adjustment. Upon consideration of Ms. Laper's response during this session, Mrs. Mc Rand decided to change her intervention approach from an insight-oriented focus to a problem-solving focus. After one day, Mrs. Mc Rand called Ms. Laper and asked her about scheduling another appointment.

Mrs. Mc Rand: Hello, this is Mrs. Mc Rand. How are you doing?

Ms. Laper: Hi, I'm O.K., but I'm kind of busy.

Mrs. Mc Rand: Can I please have about five minutes of your time?. If this is a bad time, maybe you could give me a better time when I could call you back.

Ms. Laper: Well, I guess that I could spare five minutes. What is it?

Mrs. Mc Rand: I would like to continue working with you and your family, and I would like to apologize for ignoring what you really wanted to talk about at your last session.

Ms. Laper: Yeah, thanks. I didn't mean to be rude, but this move has been hard on all of us, not just Casey. It just didn't seem like we were accomplishing anything at all.

Mrs. Mc Rand: That's true, all of you are going through a difficult adjustment. How can I be of help?

Ms. Laper: Well, you can help me to start looking for a new place, and I will need a new job. And for the kids, I was thinking that it might be better if I could find some way to keep them busy so that they didn't have to spend so much time cramped up in this place.

Mrs. Mc Rand: Those are great ideas. Would you like to involve all of the children in a family session so that we can talk about these things. I could also involve our case manager in part of the session so that she can give you some leads on housing and jobs.

Ms. Laper: That might work.

Although she was hesitant, Ms. Laper agreed to meet with Mrs. Mc Rand again. The focus of this session was discuss how they could help each other deal with their eviction and to support the family in finding resources and ideas to help them to deal with and overcome this problem. Ms. Laper and her five children (Casey, 12; Tracy, 10; Brittany, 7; Marc; 5 and Ed, 2) attended the session. Mrs. Mc Rand began by providing toys to keep Marc and Ed busy; and by engaging the family members in a discussion about how they were dealing with being at their Aunt Sylvia and Unlce Roy's.

Mrs. Mc Rand: I'm glad that all of you could make it. Maybe we can start by talking about how each of you is dealing with being at your relatives' house.

Ms. Laper: Well, I felt really guilty about us having to go there, and I want to start by telling all of you guys that I am sorry, and that I will do something about finding another place for us.

Mrs. Mc Rand: That's a big part of the reason that your mother brought everyone here today. I'm going to introduce you to Ms. Jacob. She is going to work together with us to help your mom find a new house and a new job.

Casey: I know that you're sorry mom, and I haven't been dealing with things too well. Uncle Roy just seems so bossy to me. He tells me what to do all the time and it makes me mad.

Ms. Laper: I know that you were used to helping me enforce the rules at our house, and now Uncle Roy has his own rules, but you have to respect him.

Tracy: It's just so crowded in there, mom. We all get on each other's nerves.

Brittany: We even have to wait to go to the bathroom.

Ms. Laper: I know that it has been hard on you guys, and that's why I am going to work on finding a new place; but until then we have to learn how to handle things.

Mrs. Mc Rand: Does anybody have any ideas about how to handle things until you get your new place?

As a result of Mrs. Mc Rand's initiation of the problem-solving process, the family began brainstorming a list of ideas about how they could cope with being at Aunt Slyvia's and Uncle Roy's. Then, they voted on the best ideas: Having a family session with Aunt Sylvia, Uncle Roy, and their cousins; finding after-school activities for the children so that they could not get tired of staying in the house; establishing house rules; limiting time in the bathroom; and using the library for one hour each day as a quiet place for the older children to do their homework.

Mrs. Mc Rand introduced the case manager, Ms. Jacob, who spent time talking with Ms. Laper about housing and job options. At the end of this meeting, Mrs. Laper told Mrs. Mc Rand that she felt as is they had actually accomplished something; and she admitted that she was pleasantly surprised. Mrs. Mc Rand found that the problem-solving approach was more relevant to the family's needs than the insight-oriented approach that she applied earlier. Rather than focusing just on Casey as the consumer, the focus was on the entire family and would also include the extended family. Since the family members were actively involved in the problem-solving process, they would be eager to try their new ideas. The focus was on new behavior and current problems rather than on underlying motives which might be confusing and frustrating for families in times of immediate need for help.

Crisis Intervention

Crises are dangerous times for families, yet, when a family crisis is effectively managed by a worker, such an intervention may gain family trust, thus leading to engagement (Goldenberg & Goldenberg, 1991). When focusing on family crisis in work with the low-income, urban, African-American, it is, of course, important to consider that many families have had direct or indirect negative experiences with social agencies and their staff ; and thus, they may feel skeptical regarding social work services (Daly, Jennings, Beckett, & Leashore, 1995; Pinderhughes, 1982; Hines & Boyd-Franklin, 1990). Often, African-American families tend to perceive therapy as a process "for crazy people" (Hines & Boyd-Franklin, 1982), and consequently, will seek such services only after all other sources of aid and support have been exhausted (Hines & Boyd-Franklin, 1982; Boyd-Franklin, 1990). Such a delay in obtaining services may increase the severity of the problems experienced and the services needed. In addition, regardless of whether the families enter therapy in crisis, family workers will need to utilize crisis intervention skills many times during the service delivery process since facilitating change almost invariably creates stress and crisis within the family (Steele & Raider, 1991). A family crisis should not be defined simply as an event, but rather, as each family's perception and reaction to an event which the family views as dangerous and threatening and over which the family has little or no control (Steele & Raider, 1991). When families feel that they cannot resolve a threat facing them, they enter a crisis state which is characterized by desperation. Since this state is quite intense, the family may latch onto whatever promises to alleviate their fear and anxiety. Initially, family members may deal with crisis by acting out or by avoiding the crisis. However, working through a crisis presents the opportunity for change and the development of new, more effective coping skills (Raider & Steele, 1991).

Social workers must consider the source of the crisis at hand and tailor the intervention to the needs presented by the crisis. The worker may ask: Has the crisis been brought about by lack of money? For example, is the family in crisis because their heat is going to be turned off on a cold winter day and they are unsure where they will go to keep warm? The family worker may consider the possibility that the crisis may be related to living in an urban area, and perhaps more specifically to concerns regarding safety: A family in which a teenage child's friend has recently been shot and killed may suffer from trauma, grief, and loss issues as well as intensified fear associated with the obvious threat in the community. Another sort of crisis may be precipitated by issues which relate to African-American ethnicity such as racism or discrimination. It is also important to consider that any crisis may be generated by a combination of all of these sources.

Families most often respond to crises such as these by engaging in self-defeating behaviors (Steele & Raider, 1991). For example, a family that has refused to talk about the shooting and death of a family friend among themselves because such discussion creates too much emotional pain and avoids confrontation of this issue. The avoidance of this confrontation is the self-defeating behavior. The goal of crisis intervention is to replace self-defeating and self-destructive behaviors with effective and adaptive coping skills which reduce the family's anxiety and enhance the family's ability to manage successfully the immediate crisis as well as possible future crises. Families in crisis feel unsure of what is happening and why. Thus, individual members may think that their reactions are not natural, thoughts that only add to each family member's fear of losing control. The worker may need to label and discuss feelings among family members in order to assist each member in identifying his/her feelings. Once feelings are recognized and acknowledged, the worker may promote active discussion and expression of these feelings. When the family achieves this task, members can regain mastery over the feelings which have precipitated the crisis state (Raider & Steele, 1991).

Crises are time-limited. The state of an active crisis usually lasts no longer than four to six weeks (Golan, 1969; Hirschowitz, 1973); although, if the crisis goes unresolved, the family may require a more intense approach (Fraser, Percora, Haapala, 1991). Family preservation services share many of the same components of the family-centered practice model discussed, although services are more intense. Family workers spend eight to ten hours per week with each family and about 60% of each worker's time is spent in direct face-to-face contact with the families (Fraser, Pecora and Haapala, 1991).

Case Illustration

Strategy: Crisis intervention may be used to engage families in services.

The Pryer family was well known to social workers at Ryan Behavioral Services. Several workers from different types of programs had worked with the family and each time the family either withdrew from services by the mother, Mrs. Pryer's, choice or their cases were discharged due to inconsistency with appointments. Mrs. Pryer, age 27, was separated from her husband of 10 years and currently caring for her 7 children alone. Mrs. Pryer's children ranged in age from 14 to 1 year old: Marx, 14; Evan, 12; Lila, 10; Mila, 9; Kesia, 7; Fresia, 4; and Aron, 1. The Pryers had moved four times since their first contact with the agency; and their phone number was often disconnected or changed. The social workers at this agency knew that this family was in need of help, but staying

126

connected with them was often a problem. One October morning, Mrs. Pryer called the Ryan Behavioral Center in crisis. "They're going to take my kids away if I don't get help right away. I've worked with you guys before and I didn't know who else to call," she stated. Mrs. Pryer went on to explain that her son, Evan, was kicked out of school that afternoon for fighting. The teacher and principal at school told Mrs. Pryer that they "had had it with Evan's continuous fighting and lack of improvement this year" and that Evan could not return to school until Mrs. Pryer had proof that he was in counseling. Mrs. Pryer came to pick Evan up from school as requested by the principal, Mrs. Colby. Due to having problems with getting the younger children ready to leave with her, Mrs. Pryer arrived later than expected at Evan's school. Mrs. Colby expressed concerns about Mrs. Pryor's ability to care for her children and stated that she was considering calling Protective Services.

During the phone call, Mrs. Pryer vented and Ms. Venton, the social worker took the call, actively listened and providing support. After listening, she directed the conversation toward the discussion of the choices that Mrs. Pryer would have to make. She allowed Mrs. Pryer to take control while also providing support and guidance.

Mrs. Pryer: I'm so confused. They say that they are going to call Protective Services on me if I don't get some help, but I've been trying to get help, and even when the kids were going to counseling, they were still getting in trouble in school. Your therapists didn't seem to get to the root of the problem and now my kids and I are in trouble; and the teachers don't seem to know what they're doing either. Their only answer is to get rid of Evan and send him home. What if I go through counseling again and I have the same problems? They'll take my kids away and make me look like a criminal.

Ms. Venton: Mrs. Pryer, you're so afraid that someone from Evan's school is going to call Protective Services. You're afraid that everyone is going to blame

127

you and call you a bad mother. You are confused, but maybe if you tell me some of the reasons why counseling didn't work out for you in the past, you and I can come up with some ways to make counseling work for you this time.

Mrs. Pryer: Well, first of all, I tried some program where I had to bring the kids to your offices. I didn't come a lot of the time because I cannot drive and the only way for we to get to the agency was by cab or bus. Ever tried riding a bus with seven children. It's a disaster! I must say, though, that I did like getting out of the house despite the trouble. I get so isolated sometimes.

Ms. Venton: It sounds like you were in our Child and Family Outpatient Program, Mrs. Pryer.

Mrs. Pryer: Yes, you're right. That was it at first. I tried the program where someone comes to the home too. That worked a little better, but then I had my phone cut off and then I had to move and we lost touch. I will admit that at that time so much had went wrong in my life that I was just tried of counseling, so I didn't make any attempts to call you guys back. Things just didn't seem to get any better, and I decided that maybe I could just make a fresh start on my own, and maybe I was right. Look at how I'm being treated: My husband leaves me; I go to Department of Social Services to get help so that I can feed my kids, and they give me barely enough to get by; and then, this crazy principal wants to take all my kids away! What more can be taken from me?

Ms. Venton: It sounds like you have a lot going on in your life.

Mrs. Pryer: Yes, I just can't handle it all by myself anymore, and no one seems to want to help me.

Ms. Venton: What kind of help do you think would be best for you and your family?

Mrs. Pryer: We need someone who can work with those people at school, and help me to explain our situation. We don't have transportation, so someone who could come to our house would be good.

Ms. Venton: Do you remember if you worked with a case manager before?

128

Mrs. Pryer: Oh yeah, that was the man that helped us with some repairs on the house. We don't need too many house repairs right now, but I remember him saying that he might be able to help with getting me connected with child care and some after-school activities for the children.

Ms. Venton: Based on what you've told me, it seems like our home-based program might work best for you, and it seems like you might also benefit from the help of a case manager.

Mrs. Pryer: You seem like you understand pretty well and I have already told you all about my family, is there any chance that you could work with us?

Ms. Venton: Yes, fortunately, I work in the home-based program. Did you work with a case manager named Mr. Trith?

Mrs. Pryer: Yes, that was his name.

Ms. Venton: Well, he still works here and he is available. Would you like to have his services as well as mine?

Mrs. Pryer: That would be good because if ever you're not available when I have a problem I could also let him know about it.

Ms. Venton: That's good thinking and remember that if neither one of us is available, you will always have the beeper number of a social worker who is on call in case of emergencies.

Mrs. Pryer: Oh, you guys didn't do that before.

Mrs. Venton: Right, this is something that we have found that most of consumers wanted and needed so it's a relatively new service.

Mrs. Pryer: I would like to be in the home-based program again, and I need help as soon as possible, so is there any thing else that I have to do?

Ms. Venton: Well, now we need to arrange a time when you can spend at least one and a half hours with us so that we can do some information gathering and get you started in services.

Mrs. Pryer: Since I need help soon, is there any way that you could come out today? That way, I could call Evan's school and tell Mrs. Colby that I already

129

have Evan and the family in counseling, and maybe you and Mr. Trith could talk to her.

Ms. Venton: Both Mr. Trith and I have an open appointment for 1:00 p.m. today is that good for you?

Mrs. Pryer: That is good because Evan is home from school right now, but if we call and let the school know that counseling has started, they will probably allow him to go back tomorrow.

Case Illustration Discussion:

Although Mrs. Pryer and her family had some negative experiences with social agencies including the school and Ryan Behavioral Health Services, Ms. Venton was able to effectively engage Mrs. Pryer. Ms. Venton could have become frustrated with Mrs. Pryer's comments about "your therapists who didn't seem to get to the root of the problem", but she understood that it was typical for someone in crisis to blame others for problems. Ms. Venton's ability to remain calm and to restate what Mrs. Pryer had just said was the first step toward the engagement process since Ms. Venton was letting Mrs. Pryer know that she heard her.

Ms. Venton also considered that Mrs. Pryer had had negative experiences with social agencies in the past, so she understood that Mrs. Pryer was skeptical. Knowing this, Ms. Venton asked questions in order to obtain information about why counseling did not work in the past. Mrs. Pryer's responses to these questions led Ms. Venton to conclude that the home-based program was most successful in serving this family, but she noted that the home-based team would have to work hard to keep Mrs. Pryer motivated. One way of doing this would be to constantly be aware of the family's needs and work toward goals that were consistent with the family's frame of reference. Ms. Venton also noted that Mrs. Pryer had tried to take care of things by herself, and it seemed that Mrs. Pryer was unsure whether social services could really be beneficial to her. In this case, the

Ms. Venton could easily identify the source of the crisis. Evan's suspension from school and the threat of Protective Service involvement prompted the crisis state for Mrs. Pryer. Mrs. Pryer responded to the crisis by blaming others. Ms. Venton knew that this behavior was typical of someone who felt that everything was being taken from her, and thus, felt out of control. To begin to diffuse this crisis, Ms. Venton tried to build on positive experiences and things that Mrs. Pryer seemed comfortable with. Fortunately, she was able to accommodate Mrs. Pryer's need to get immediate help. Ms. Venton's inclusion of Mr.Trith was also helpful since he was a familiar person with whom Mrs. Pryer seemed comfortable. Through the course of the conversation, Ms. Venton was able to establish good rapport with Mrs. Pryer. Ms. Venton knew that she had done a good job of establishing rapport when Mrs. Pryer stated that "You seem like you understand pretty well and I have already told you all about my family, is there any chance that you could work with us?". Ms. Venton successfully engaged Mrs. Pryer using crisis intervention. The next task for Ms. Venton and Mr. Trith and Ms. Venton would be to further engage the family using an ethnic sensitive engagement process.

Reframing

Reframing is referred to as relabeling the symptoms in the Structural school. By giving a symptom another name, it opens alternate structural pathways for family members to deal with one another around the issue. The Strategic school labels this as method positive interpretation which basically ascribes positive motives to consumers. The reason for this is that blaming, criticism, and negative terms tend to mobilize resistance as family members organize their defensive energies to disown the perjoritive label.

For many low-income, African-American families, symptoms are most productively reframed as helping the family adapt to changes. Changes can be viewed in terms of the family moving through the life cycle and/or environmental changes. For example, one may reframe a young child's disruptive behavior and failing grades in school as the child's way of attention seeking to bring Mom and Grandmother closer together to help the family adjust to the older child leaving home to live on his own. One might also suggest that the younger child's behavior is a response to the stress the family is experiencing as a result of the older child going off to live on his own.

Functional family therapists describe positive reframing as relabeling. From the functional perspective, family members cannot change their behavior until they change their view of themselves and other family members. Relabeling is regarded as a message that "relevances" behavior for family members. For example, one might reframe grandmother's over intrusiveness into the privacy of her daughter to be an expression of grandmother's caring and protectiveness. Relabeling can also help family members to view others as they would like to see them. For example, one might relabel a son's extreme passivity as a striving to become the ideal son who always minds his mother.

Reframing has a number of facets or variations. One variation is defining problems of one or two members of the family as interactional. This helps the family to view the problem as shared rather than one which can be blamed on one or two people. For example, a family where Father is rarely home because of his work schedule, Mother is overwhelmed and helpless and Daughter pursues relationships with boys who are gang members, one might say, "Daughter initiates relationships with boys who are troublemakers to help Mom deal with her loneliness. When Daughter goes out with gang members, Mom gets overwhelmed and thus, Dad spends more time at home."

Absolving blame is another dimension of reframing. For example, one might remark that Mom's extremely protective behavior is like that of her mother and grandmother and has been helpful in maintaining family life for generations, both on the farm in Alabama as well as upon relocation to the city. Mom is in fact fulfilling a family script as well as a script that reflects parental concern for children that is based on African-American values. Another approach is to confirm

132

existence of an obviously negative characteristic of a family member while at the same time absolving that family member of blame for that characteristic. For example, one might emphasize that alcoholism is a disease, something some people have no control over, similar to diabetes. Therefore, although Dad's alcoholism has created a tremendous financial burden on the family it is not a sign of moral weakness.

Case Illustration

Fifteen-year-old Monique blamed her mother, Mrs. Taylor, for her aggressive behaviors toward Mrs. Taylor at home. Five months before the worker's meeting with the Taylors, Monique was out walking in her inner-city neighborhood when an adult male called to her. Monique stated that she was afraid not to answer his call because, "He was bigger than me, and I didn't know what he'd do." The man took Monique into an abandoned house and raped her. Monique survived the experience and ran back home. She was able to tell her mother about the rape a few days later. Mrs. Taylor believed Monique, but the two were unable to talk openly about this incident. According to Mrs. Taylor, Monique immediately began to act in a promiscuous manner. Mrs Taylor identified specific behaviors that she considered promiscuous. She stated that Monique had begun to attempt to date men much older than herself, (aged 20-30), and that Monique was often interested in what material items (jewelry, money, etc.) the men might give her. Mrs. Taylor expressed concern, observing again that these behaviors began to occur only after Monique was raped. Mrs. Taylor attempted to keep Monique at home as much as possible in order to protect her. For many years, the Taylors had been active members of Calvary Baptist Church. Mrs. Taylor stated that she had relied on support from her church as she faced the struggles of being a single-mother. She began to lecture Monique as to how getting more involved in church would help her. Monique then shared her frustrations with the family worker.

Monique: She drives me crazy. The mean things I do to her are her fault.

133

She asks for it. I want to go out and have fun like other kids and she tries to make me stay in the house all the time. Then she makes me even crazier with all her religious talk. I can't stand it.

(Mrs. Taylor becomes tearful.)

Mrs. Taylor: You were raped, Monique. That should tell you that the neighborhood is not safe for young girls! And another thing is that our religion has helped us to survive; we can't let go of that now.

Monique: See how crazy she is.

Worker: What I see is not a crazy mother. I see a mother who is caring and concerned, who wants to protect you.

The family worker's response demonstrated use of the reframing method. Rather than allowing Monique to see her mother as a woman who lectures, nags, and drives Monique crazy, the worker characterized Mrs. Taylor's behavior as that of a caring, concerned parent. Monique's tendency to rebel against her religion was confirmed as typical of healthy adolescent development. The worker assisted the family in setting manageable goals; and it was planned that progress regarding these goals would be discussed at the next family meeting.

Mrs. Taylor and Monique agreed to utilize coping skills such as anger management techniques: Monique agreed to take a deep breath and count to ten when her mom began to lecture. She would then proceed to calmly ask her mother to stop lecturing. Mrs. Taylor agreed to stop when she was asked in a calm manner. She also agreed to let Monique go on one approved outing with a friend that week. The worker told Mrs. Taylor and Monique that they could call her (the worker) to let her know about any progress or struggles. Both Monique and her mother agreed that they would call the worker as the need arose. It was confirmed that Mrs. Taylor's religious beliefs were important to her, and she later found it helpful to attend a parent support group offered at her church. As communication skills were nurtured, Mrs. Taylor and Monique were able to talk about the rape more openly, exploring the traumatic impact in greater depth.

Encouraging Systems Anxiety

With some low income African-American families it may be necessary to create significant systems anxiety before they are ready to examine their own dynamics and move toward change. Charles Whitiker (1981) advocates two approaches to increase systems anxiety. The first involves suggesting that the family bring in or permit the worker to consult with as many generations in the family as possible with particular emphasis on bringing in grandparents and extended family in treatment. This approach is particularly useful with low-income, African-American families who maintain a strong tie with extended family and perceive significant responsibility to grandparents and extended family. Acceptance of this responsibility and obligation is a function of both African-American values and culture.

Whitiker (1981) also suggests that involving two professionals in the session increases the power of the professionals exponentially. If the family is active in a Black Church, it may be useful to invite a clergyman to participate in treatment as a co-therapist, providing the clergyman is supportive of the idea. In such a situation, the clergy's religious or moral presence directly increases the power of the therapist and may significantly elevate the family's system anxiety hopefully leading to change. Obviously, such a strategy cannot be undertaken without both the worker and clergyman exploring each other's views and approaches to determine if they could indeed participate in therapy together. It may be necessary to encourage systemic anxiety to help some low-income African-American families confront their own dynamics and move toward change.

Network Therapy

An approach to family change particularly well suited to low-income African-American families is network therapy (Rveneni, 1979, Speck, Atteneave, 1973). Family network therapy seeks to assemble together the resources of family, extended family, friends, neighbors, and congregations in order to respond to families in disequilibrium due to extreme stress overload. These individuals and groups in the family's network serve as supports, resources, advisors, and problem-solvers to the family during times of crisis. Techniques used in family network therapy sessions as quite similar to group work techniques. Members of Church congregations are logical participants in network therapy for religious families. Such a group is usually quite acceptable to the family and already comfortable with each other, having participated in religious ceremonies in the past. Further, the presence of fellow congregants and clergy provide a religious valence in the network sessions which often provides the family with additional motivation to complete tasks and move on suggestions which are proposed in the network sessions. Network therapy may be an effective approach for some low-income African-American families comprised of extensive extended families.

Summary of Treatment Strategies Effective with Low-Income Urban, African-American Families

- Introduce yourself by sharing your background and some information about how you work. Personalize the relationship to the extent the client finds out about an interesting facet in your life.

- Do not focus directly on the problem. Use professional self-disclosure to build a relationship.

- Find a common ground for conversation with the family so that it can serve as a bridge between you.

- Become a human being to your clients by expressing humor or sharing a brief story about yourself.

- The worker should function in the inquirer and learner role while the family is in the teaching and clarifying role.

- Provide at least two sessions to build rapport. Low-income, African-American families instinctively search for inner qualities of the worker. Finding these traits the consumer begins to lower his or her resistance and opens up to the worker. If not, clients will maintain resistance and drop out after the initial session or will seek another worker.

- Put the family at ease by offering modest refreshments.

- Ask the client how he or she feels about coming to the first session.

- Alternate between open and closed questions.

- Convey facts readily.

- Offer opinions and ideas that will increase knowledge of the situation.

- Move slowly toward reaching for feelings.

- Be alert to the client's use of language to label and categorize a problem.

- Be sure to ask about family, spouse, extended family, neighbors, the church community.

- Check out availability of churches and other community resources to facilitate development of intervention strategies.

- Identify natural helping resources that the family uses in its search for help.
- Ascertain link between individual functioning and the family, community, church.
- Be alert to families' cultural criteria for determining problem resolution.
- Establish intermediate, small goals with low-income, urban African-American families so that when these are achieved, uncertainty about therapy is reduced and motivation increases.
- Reframe symptoms as helping the family adapt to its environment.
- Reframe symptoms as something over which family members have no control rather than a sign of moral weakness.
- To establish systems anxiety with religious families, consult with or involve clergy and/or extended family in treatment.
- Involve clergy in the treatment process with religious families by providing assurance that the religious values and beliefs of families will be respected and clergy will be consulted on questions of theology.
- Work through clergy to help obtain resources for religious families in need.
- Identify and suggest that religious families participate in church based self-help groups, socialization groups, classes and other activities as appropriate.
- Avoid using labels and diagnoses in the case record before you have had ample opportunity assess the family yourself.
- Engage low-income, African-American families in settings in which they are comfortable and which are close to home.
- Build on family strengths with regard to family structure, family functioning and environment coping throughout the treatment process.
- Goals should be attainable, specific, observable and measurable.
- For most low-income, African-American families the first treatment priority should be the family's concrete needs (often referred to as case management).

- Utilize a problem-solving approach to clinical work with African-American families. Put off until later in the treatment process, or avoid entirely, insight oriented or feelings centered techniques.

- Utilize family systems, behavioral, social learning and cognitive behavioral strategies and techniques to help the family change.

- Utilize crisis intervention as an opportunity to gain the family's trust.

- Invest time and energy to become familiar with the history, culture and values of low-income, urban, African-American families.

- The most effective way to do a family assessment for low-income African-American families is by making a home visit.

References

Ak'bar, N. (1984). Afrocentric social services for human liberation. Journal of Black Studies, 14, p. 395-414.

Allen, W.R. (1981). "Moms, dads, and boys: Race and sex differences in the socialization of male children." In L.E. Gary (Ed.), Black men, (pp. 99-114). Beverly Hills, CA: Sage Publications.

Allen-Meares, P. & Burman, S. (1995). "The endangerment of African American men: An appeal for social work action." Social Work, 40, (2), pp. 268-274.

Anderson, J. (1992). Family centered practice in the 1990s: A multicultural perspective. Journal of Multicultural Social Work, 1, (4), p. 17-28.

Anderson, J.D. (1988). The education of Blacks in the South, 1860-1935, Chapel Hill: University of North Carolina Press.

Aponte, H.J. (1991). "Training on the person of the therapist for work with the poor and minorities." In K.G. Lewis (Ed.) Family systems application to social work: Training and clinical practice, (pp. 23-39). Binghamton, New York: Haworth Press.

Asante, K. A. (1988). Afrocentricity. Trenton, N. J.: Africa World.

Armbruster, P., Gerstein, & Fallon, T. (1997). "Bridging the gap between service need and service utilization: A school-based mental health program. Community Mental Health Journal, 33, (3), p. 199-211.

Bacca Zin, M. & Eitzen, D. (1993). Diversity in families, (third edition). New York: Harper Collins.

Bagley, C.H. & Carroll, J. (1995). "Healing forces in African-American families." In H.I. Cubbin, E.A. Thompson, A.I. Thompson & J.A. Futrell (Eds.), Resiliency in ethnic minority families: African-American families, volume 2, (pp. 117-142). Madison, Wisconsin: University of Wisconsin System.

Bagley & Thomas, E.J. (1978). Generating innovation in social work: The paradigm of development research," Journal of Social Science Research, (2), p. 20.

Baldwin, S. (1985). The costs of caring: Families with disabled children. London: Routledge & Kegan Paul.

Bingham, R. & Guinyard, J. (1982, August). Counseling black women: Recognizing societal scripts. Paper presented at the 90th Meeting of the American Psychological Association.

Barthel, J. (1992a). "Family preservation, value, and beliefs." Youth Policy, 14, (6), p. 32-36.

Barthel, J. (1992b). "For Children's Sake: The Promise of family preservation." New York: Annie E. Casey Foundation, Edna McConnell Clark Foundation for Child Development, and Skillman Foundation.

Barbarin, O.A. (1993). "Coping and resilience: Exploring the inner lives of African-American children." Journal of Black Psychology, 19, p. 478-492.

Barrett, R. K. (1991). "Homicide and Suicide: Who is at Risk?" The American Black Male. New York: William Pruitt Enterprises.

Bascom, W. (1969). The Yoruba of Southwestern Nigeria. New York: Rinehart and Winston.

Beck, A.T. (1976). Cognitive therapy and emotional disorders. New York: International Universities Press.

Beckett, J.O. & Coley, S. (1987). Ecological intervention: A case example with a Black family. Journal of Counseling and Human Service Professionals, 2, p. 1-18.

Beverly, C. (1995). "Spirituality: OFT The missing link in African-American family therapy." Detroit, Michigan: Wayne State University.

The Black Community Crusade for Children, coordinated by the Children's Defense Fund. Progress and Peril: Black Children in America. (1993). Children's Defense Fund: Washington, DC.

Billingsley, A. (1992). Climbing Jacob's Ladder: The enduring legacy of African American families: Simon and Schuster.

Billingsley, A. (1968). Black families in white America. Englewood Cliffs, N.J.: Prentice Hall.

Billingsley, A. (1989, May). The Black church as a social service institution. Paper presented at a National Symposium of Grant Makers.

Boyd-Franklin, N. (1990). Empowering Black families in therapy. Washington, D.C.: American Association for Marriage and Family Therapy.

Boyd-Franklin, N. (1989). Black Families in therapy: A multisystemic approach. New York: Guilford Press.

Boyd-Franklin, N. (1987). "The contribution of family therapy models to the treatment of Black families." Psychotherapy, 24, (3-s), p. 621-629).

Braithwaite, R.L. (1981). Interpersonal relationships between Black males and Black females. In L.E. Gard (Ed.) Black men, (pp. 83-97). Beverley Hills, CA: Sage Publications.

Burton, L. & Bengston, V. (1985). Black grandmothers: Issues of timing and continuity of roles. In V. Bengston & J. Robertson (Eds.), Grandparenthood, (p. 61-78). Beverly Hills, CA: Sage Publications.

Busch, K.G., Zagar, R, Hughes, J. R., Arbit, J., Bussell, R. E., (1990). "Adolescents who kill," Journal of Clinical Psychology, 46, (4), p. 473-485.

Chestnag, L.W. (1972). Character development in a hostile society. Occasional Paper #3, Chicago, Illinois: University of Chicago.

Chilman, C.S. (1966, January). "Social work practice with very poor families: Some implications suggested by the available research." Welfare in Review, 4, (1), p. 13-22.

Coley, S.M. & Beckett, J.O. "Black battered women, Practice issues," Social Casework, 69, p. 483-490.

Comer, J. (1980). The black family: An adaptive perspective. In M. Fantini & R. Cardenas (Eds.), Parenting in a Multicultural Society (p. 43-53). New York: Longman.

Curtis, L. (1975). Violence, race and culture, Lexington, MA: Lexington Books.

Daly, A., Jennings, J., Beckett, J.O. & Leashore, B.R. (1995). "Effective coping strategies of African-Americans." Social Work, 40, (2), p. 145-288.

142

Davis, K., Lillie-Blanton, M., Mullan, F., Powe, N., & Rowland, D., (1989). Health care for Black Americans: The public sector role. In D. Willis (Ed.), Health Policies and Black Americans, (pp. 213-248). New Jersey: Transaction Publishers.

Davis, L. (1993). Black and Single: Meeting and choosing a partner who's right for you. Noble Press.

Davis, K., Lillie-Blanton, M., Lyons, B., Mullan, F., Powe, N., & Rowland, D. (1989). "Health care for Black Americans: The publilc sector role." In D. Willis, (Ed.), Health policies and Black Americans (p. 213-248). New Jersey: Transaction Publishers.

DeLaCancela, V. (1994). "Coolin': The psychosocial communication of African & Latino men," In African American Males: A critical link in the African American family, Dionne J. Jones (Ed.) (1994). New Brunswick, New Jersey, Transaction Publishers.

Downs, S. Whitelaw. (1994). Skillman Center for Children: Neighborhood-based family support. Detroit: Wayne State University, Skillman Center for Children.

Drake, S & Cayton, H. (1945). Black metropolis. New York: Harcourt, Brace, & World.

Driver, D. E. (1992). Defending the left: An individual's guide to fighting for social justice, individual rights, and the environment. Noble Press.

Elwood, D. & Crane, J. (1990). Journal of Economic Perspectives, 4, (4), (Fall).

Farrar, E. & Connolly, C. (1991). Improving middle schools in Boston: A report on Boston Compact and school distract initiatives. Educational Policy, 5, (1), p. 4-28.

Flaherty, L.T., Weist, M.D., & Warner, B. (1996). "School-based mental health services in the United States: History, current models, and needs," Community Mental Health Journal, 32, (4).

Fine, M., Schwebal, A. I. & James-Meyers, L. (1987). Family stability in Black families: Values underlying three different perspectives. Journal of Comparative Studies, 14, (2), p. 201-232.

First, M.B., M.D., (1994). Diagnostic and statistical manual of mental disorders.

143

Washington, DC: American Psychiatric Association.

Foley, V. (1975). "Family therapy with Black disadvantage families: Some observations on roles, communications, and techniques. Journal of Marriage and Family Counseling, 1, p. 29-38.

Foster, H.J. (1983). African patterns in the African-American family. Journal of Black Studies, 14, (2), p. 201-232.

Frankel, H. (1988). Family-centered, home-based services in child protection: A review of the Research. Social Services Review, 62, p. 137-157.

Franklin, A.J. (1989). "Therapeutic interventions with urban Black adolescents," In R.L. Jones (Ed.), Black adolescents. p. 309-337. Berkeley, CA: Cobb & Henry.

Franklin, C. & Streeter, C.L. (1995). "School reform: Linking public services with human services." Social Work, 40, p. 773-782.

Fraser, M. & Haapala, D. (1987-1988). "Home-based family treatment: A Quantitative-Qualitative Assessment." Journal of Applied Social Sciences, 12, (Fall-Winter 1987-1988), p. 1-23.

Fraser, M.W., Pecora, P.J., & Haapala, D.A. (1991). Families in crisis. New York: Walter de Gruyter, Inc.

Frazier, E. F. (1969). The Negro family in the United States. Chicago:University of Chicago Press.

Frazier, E. F. (1961). Black Bourgeoisie. New York: Macmillian Co.

Gary, L. (1981). Black Men . Sage Publications: Newbury Park: California

Gary, L. E. & Leashore, B. R. (1982). High-risk status of black men. Social Work, 27 , p. 54-58.
Gaw, A. (1982). Cross cultural psychiatry. Boston: John Wright.

Genovese, E. D. (1974). Roll, Jordan, roll. New York: Patheon Books.

Gleick, J. (1987). Chaos: Making a new science. New York: Viking Press.

Geismar, L.L. & Krisberg, J. 91967). The forgotten neighborhood: Site of an early skirmish in the war on poverty. Metuch, N.J.: Scarecrow Press.

Gibbs, J. T. (1989). "Black adolescents and youth: An update on an endangered species", In R. J. Jones (Ed). Black adolescents, p.3-28, Berkeley, CA: Cobb & Henry.

Golan, N. (1969, July). "When is a client in crisis?" Social Casework, p. 389-394.

Goldenberg, J.R. (1993). "Is multicultural therapy in sight?" Family Therapy News, 24, (1), p. 7-8; 16.

Goldenberg, I. & Goldenberg, H. (1991). Family therapy: An overview. Pacific Grove, California: Brooks/Cole Publishing Co.

Green, J. (1982). Cultural awareness in the human services. New Jersey: Prentice-Hall.

Grier, W. J. & Cobbs, P.M. (1968). Black rage. New York: Basic Books.

Grier , W. J. & Cobbs, P. M. (1980). Black Rage. New York: Basic Books Inc.

Haapala, D. A. (1983). Perceived helpfulness, attributed critical incident responsibility and a discrimination of home-based family therapy treatment outcome: Homebuilders Model. Report prepared for the Department of Health and Human Services, Administration for Children, Youth, and Families, Behavioral Sciences Institute, Federal Way, Washington.

Halper, G. & Jones, M.A. (1981). Serving families at risk of dissolution: Public preventive services in New York City. New York: City of New York Human Resources Administration.

Hare, N. & Hare, J. (1984). The Endangered black family: Coping with the unisexualization and coming extinction of the black race. Black Think Tank: SanFrancisco, CA

Hernandez, D. (1993). America's children, resources from family, government, and the economy. New York: Russell Sage Foundation.

Hill, R. (1971). Strengths of the Black family. New York: National Urban League.

Hill, R. (1978). The strengths of Black families. New York: Emeron-Hall.

Hill, R., Foote, N., Aldous, J., Carlson, R. , & MacDonaldson, R. (1978). Family development in three generations. Cambridge, MA: Schenkman.

Hines, P.M. (1989). The family life cycle of poor Black families. In E.A. Carter & M. McGoldrick (Eds). The changing life cycle: A framework for family therapy. Boston: Allyn & Bacon.

Hines, P.M. & Boyd-Franklin, N. (1982). "Black families." In M. McGoldrick, J.K. Pearce, & J. Giordano (Eds.). Ethnicity and family therapy. New York: Guilford Press.

Hirschowitz, R.G. (1973, December). "Crisis theory: A formulation." Psychiatric Annals, 3, p. 38-47.

Ho, M.K. (1987). Family therapy with ethnic minorities. Beverly Hills, CA: Sage.

Hoffman-Graff, M.A. (1977). "Interviewer use of positive and negative self-disclosure and interviewer-subject sex pairing." Journal of Counseling Psychology, 24, p. 184-190.

Hoffman L., Wyatt, F. (1960). Social change and motivations for having larger families: Some theoretical considerations. Merill-Palmer Quarterly, 6, p. 260-271.

Houston, L.N. (1990). Psychological principles and the black experience. New York: University Press of America.

Jackson, J. (1971). Black grandparents in the south. Phylon, 32, p. 260-271.

Jones, D. (1994). African American Males: A critical link in the African American family. Transaction Publishers : New Brunswick, New Jersey.

Kaplan, L. (1986). Working with multiproblem families. Lewington, Massachusetts: Lexington Books.

Kaplan, L. & Girard, J. (1994). Strengthening high risk families. New York: Lexington Books, an imprint of Mac Millan, Inc.

Kessler, R. K., Burgess, A. W., & Douglass, J., (1990). Sexual homicide, Lexington, MA: Lexington Books.

Khoapa, W. A. (1980). The African personality. Tokyo:United Nations University.

Kinney, J., Haapala, D., & Booth (1991). Keeping families together: The Homebuilder's model. New York: Walter de Gruyter.

Kiselica, M. (1995). Multicultural counseling with teenage fathers: A practical guide. Sage Publications: Thousand Oaks, CA.

Kotlowitz, A. (1995). "Breaking the silence: Growing up in the inner-city." In H. McCubbin, E.A. Thompson, A.I. Thompson, & J.A. Futrell (Eds.). Resiliency in ethnic minority families: African American families, volume 2, (pp. 3-15). Madison, Wisconsin: University of Wisconsin System.

Leashore, B. (1981). Social services and black men. In Black Men . Sage Publications: Newbury Park: California

Leigh, J.W. & Green, J.W. (1982). "The structure of the Black community: The knowledge base for social services." In J.W. Green (Ed.). Cultural awareness in the human services. New Jersey: Prentice-Hall.

Levine, R.A. (1964, January). "Treatment in the home." Social Work, 9, 19-28.

Lewis, R. E. (1991). "What are the characteristics of intensive family services?" In M. W. Fraser, P. Pecora, & D.A. Haapala. Families in crisis: The impact of intensive family preservation services. (p. 93-107). New York: Aldine De Gruyter.

Lewin, T. (1988). " Black churches: a new mission on the family." The New York Times, August 24, A1.

Littlejohn-Blake, S.M. & Anderson-Darling, C. (1993). "Understanding the strengths of Black families." Journal of Black Studies, 23, p. 460-471.

Loeber, R., Wung, P., Keenan, K., Giroux, B., Stourhammer-Loeber, M., Van Kammen, W., & Maughan, B., (1993). Developmental pathways in disruptive child behavior. Development and psychopathology, 5, p. 103-133.

Lum, D. (1986). Social work practice with people of color. Monterey, CA: Brooks/Cole.

Madanes, C., & Haley, J. (1977). "Dimensions of family therapy." The Journal of Nervous and Mental Disease, 165, p. 88-98.

Madhubuti, H.R. (1990). Black men: Obsolete, single, dangerous. Chicago:

Third World Press.

Majors, R. (1991). "Non-verbal behaviors and communication styles among African Americans," In R. Jones (Ed.), Black Psychology, third edition, p. 269-294. Berkley, CA: Cobb & Henry.

Majors, R.G. & Billson, J.M. (Eds.) (1992). Cool Pose: The dilemmas of Black manhood in America, New York: Lexington Books

Marital status and living arrangements (1991, March). Current Population Reports, Series P-20, No. 461.

Martin, J & Martin, E. (1985) The helping tradition in the Black family and . community. National Association of Social Workers: Washington, DC.

Martin, E & Martin, J. (1978). The Black extended family. Chicago: University of Chicago Press.

Maslow, A. (1954). Motivation and personality. New York: Harper & Row.

Massachusetts Department of Social Services (1993). A family-centered approach to case management practice. Boston, MA: Massachusetts Department of Social Services.

Mbiti, J. S. (1969). African religions and philosophy. New York: Praeger.

McAdoo, H. (1995). "African-American families: Strengths and realities." In H. McCubbin, E.A. Thompson, A.I. Thompson, & J.A. Futrell (Eds.). Resiliency in ethnic minority families: African American families, volume 2, (pp. 17-30). Madison, Wisconsin: University of Wisconsin System.

Mc Adoo, H. (1989 a). Cultural issues affecting labor force participation. Investigating in people: A strategy to address Americans workforce crisis. 2, Washington, D.C. : The Congress of National Black Churches Inc.

McAdoo, H. (1989 b). Black families. New York: Sage Publications.

McAdoo, H. (1983). Societal stress: The Black family. In H. McCubbin & E. Figley. Stress and family: Coping with normative transitions, (pp. 178-187). New York: Brunner/Mazel.

McAdoo, H. & Crawford, V. (1991). "The Black church and family support programs." In D. Unger & D. G. Powell (Eds.), Families as nurturing systems: Support across the life span. (p. 193-202). New York: Haworth Press.

McAdoo, H. & Crawford, V. (1989). Project SPIRIT Evaluation Report. Washington, D.C. : The Congress of National Black Churches, Inc.

McCarthy, P. and Betz, N. (1978). "Differential effects of self-disclosing versus self-involving counselor statements." Journal of Counseling Psychology, 25, p. 479-482.

McCubbin, H.I., Thompson, E.A., Thompson, H.I., & Futrell, J.A. (1995). Resiliency in ethnic minority families, volume 2. Madison, WI: University of Wisconsin System.

McGoldrick, M., Preto, N. Garcia, Hines, P. Moore, & Lee, E. (1991). "Ethnicity and family therapy." In A.S. Gurman & D. Kniskern, Handbook of family therapy, volume II, (p. 546-582). New York: Brunner/Mazel.

McGoldrick, M., Anderson, C., & Walsh, F. (1989). Women in families: A framework for family therapy. New York: W.W. Norton.

McGoldrick, M., Pearce, J.K., Giordano, J. (1982). Ethnicity and family therapy. New York: The Guilford Press.

McKinney, G.E. (1970). "Adapting family therapy to multideficit families." Social Casework, 51, (6), p. 327-333.

Menkiti, I. A. (1984). Person and community in African traditional thought. In R.A. Wright (Ed.), African philosophy. (p. 171-181). New York: University Press of America.

Meyers, H.F. (1989). "Urban stress and mental health in Black youth: An epidemiologic and conceptual update." In R.J. Jones (Ed.). Black adolescents (p. 123-154). Berkeley, CA: Cobb & Henry.

Miller, A. T. (1993). Social science, social policy and the heritage of African American families. In M.B. Katz (Ed.). The underclass debate (p. 254-289). Princeton, NJ: Princeton University Press.

Minuchin, S. (1974). Families and family therapy. Cambridge, Mass.: Harvard University Press.

Minuchin, S., Montalvo, B., Guerney, B.G., Rosman, B.L., & Schumer, F. (1967).

149

<u>Families of the slums: An exploration fo their structure and treatment</u>. New York: Basic Books.

Morton, S. & Grigsby, K. (Eds.), (1993). <u>Advancing family preservation practice</u>. Newbury Park, CA: Sage.

Nilsson, D., Strassberg, D. & Bannon, J. (1979). "Perceptions of counselor self-disclosure: An analogy study." <u>Journal of Counseling Psychology, 26</u>, p. 399-404.

Nobles, W.W. (1972). African philosophy: Foundations for Black psychology. In R. L. Jones (Ed.), <u>Black psychology</u> (p.18-32). New York: Harper & Row.

Nobles, W. W. (1980). African American family life: An instrument of culture. In H. P. McAdoo (Ed.), <u>Black families</u> (p. 77-86). Beverly Hills, CA.: Sage Publications.

Owens, L.W. (1976). <u>This species of property</u>. New York: Oxford University Press.

Pear, R. (1991), (December 4). "Bigger number of new mothers are unmarried." <u>New York Times</u>, p. A-11.

Piatt, A.L., Ketterson, T.U., Skitka, L.J., Searight, H.R., Rogers, B.J., Reuterman, N.A., & Manley, C.M. (1993). "The relationship of psychological adjustment to perceived family functioning among African-American adolescents." <u>Adolescence, 28</u>, p. 673-684.

Pinderhughes, E. (1982). "Afro-American families and the victim system." In M. McGoldrick, J.K. Pearce, & J. Giordano (Eds.), <u>Ethnicity and family therapy</u>. New York: The Guilford Press.

Polansky, N.A., Chalmers, M.A., Buttenweiser, E., & Williams, D.P. (1981). <u>Damaged parents: An anatomy of neglect</u>. Chicago, Illinois: University of Chicago Press.

Poole, T. G. (1990). Black families and the black church: A sociohistorical perspective. In H. E. Cheatham & J. B. Stewart (Eds). <u>Black families</u>. (p. 33-48). New Brunswick, New Jersey: Transition.

Rabin, C., Sens, M., & Rosenbaum, H. (1982, October). <u>Journal of marital and family therapy, 8</u>, (4), p. 451-461.

Raider, M. (1989, May). "A two year research study on religion and family function." Unpublished manuscript, presented at The American Association for Marriage and Family Therapy: San Francisco, California.

Raider, M. (1987). "A service delivery-focused approach in evaluation of groupwork intervention in residential treatment agencies," Residential group care and treatment, vol. 6, no. 5.

Richie, B. (1981). "Black battered women: A challenge for the Black community." In I.N. Toure (Ed.), An overview of third world women and violence. Washington, D.C.: Rape and Crisis Center.

Rickely, A. & Allen, L. (1987). "Preventing maladjustment from infancy to adolescence." In A. Raxdin (Ed.), Developmental psychology and psychiatry (p. 217-232). Newbury Park, CA: Sage.

Rose, H. M. & McClain, P. D. (Eds.) (1990). Race, place and risk. New York: State University Press.

Rveneni, U. (1979). Networking families in crisis. New York: Human Sciences Press, 1979.

Sallee, A.L. & Mannes, M. (1991). Reflecting on the past, present, and future of the family preservation movement. Working Papers series 1. Las Cruces, N.M.: Family Preservation Institute, Department of Social Work, New Mexico State University.

Schiele, J.H. (1990). Organizational theory from an Afrocentric perspective. Journal of Black Studies, 21, p. 145-161.

Skinner, B.F. (1953). Science and human behavior, Macmillan.

Speck, R.V. & Atteneave, C. (1973). Family networks. New York: Vantage Books.

Staples, R. (1989). "Masculinity and race: The dual dilemma of Black men." In M. Kimmel & M. Messner, Men's lives. New York: Macmillan.

Staples, R. (1987). Black male genocide: A final solution to the race problem in America. Black Scholar, 18, (3), p. 2-11.

Staples, R. (1985). "Changes in the Black family structure: The conflict between family ideology and structural conditions. Journal of Marriage and the Family, 47, p. 1005-10013.

Simons, R.L. & Gray, P.A. (1989). "Perceived blocked opportunity as an explanation of delinquency among lower-class Black males: A research note." Journal of Research in Crime and Deliquency, 26, p. 90-101.

Smitherman, G. (1995). African American women speak out on Anita Hill - Clarence Thomas. Wayne State University Press: Detroit, MI

Spencer, M.B., Cole, S.P., Dupree, D., Glymph, A., & Pierre, P. (1993). "Self-efficacy among urban African American adolescents: Exploring issues of risk vulnerability, and resilience. Development and psychopathology, 5, p. 719-739.

Stack, C. (1974). All our kin. New York: Harper & Row.

Steele, W. (in press). Developing crisis response teams in schools. Holmes, FL: Learning Publications.

Steele, W. Raider, M. (1991). Working with families in crisis: School-based intervention, The Guilford Press.

Stewart, R. (1990). Familial satisfaction among African-Americans. Unpublished doctoral dissertation, Howard University, Washington, D.C.

Taylor, R., Chatters, L., Tucker, M., & Lewis, E. (1990). Black families. Journal of Marriage and the Family, 52, p. 993-1014.

Timberlake, E. & Chipungu, S. (1992). Contemporary meaning among African-American middle-class grandmothers, Journal of the National Association of Social Workers, 37, (3), p. 216-222.

Thomas, E.J. (1992). The design and development model of practice research. In Research utilization in the social services, Grasso, A. J., & Epstein, I, Eds. Binghamton, New York: Haworth Press.

Thomas, E.J. (1978a). Generating innovation in social work: The paradigm of developmental research. Journal of Social Service Research, 2, p. 95-116.

Thomas, E. J. (1978b). Mousetraps, developmental research, and social work education. Social Service Review, 52, p. 468-483.

Thornton, M.C. (1995). "Indigenous resources and strategies of resistance: Informal caregiving and racial socialization in Black communities." In H.I. McCubbin, E.A. Thompson, A.I. Thompson & J.A. Futrell, Resiliency in ethnic minority families: African-American families. Madison, Wisconsin: The University of Wisconsin System.

Tucker, B. & Mitchell-Kerna, C. (1985). "Sex ratio imblance among African-Americans: Conceptual and methodological issues." In R. Jones (Ed.), Advances in Black psychology, volume 1. Berkeley, CA: Cobb & Henry.

Ullmann, L.P. & Krosner, L. (1965). Case studies in behavior modification. Holt, Rinehart & Winston.

United States Bureau of the Census (1989). "Statistical Abstract of the United States," (109th ed.). Washington, D.C.: U.S. Government Printing Office.

Van Meter, M.J.S. (1986). "An alternative to foster care for victims of child abuse/neglect: A university-based program." Child Abuse and Neglect, 10, p. 79-84.

Vontress, C. (1973). Racial differences: Impediments to rapport. In J. Goodman (Ed.), Dynamics of racism in social work practice (pp. 80-89). Washington, D.C.: National Association of Social Workers.

Washington, Elise B. (1996). The Uncivil War: The struggle between Black men and women. Chicago: The Nobel Press.

Wasik, B.H., Bryant, D.M. & Lyons, C.M. (1990). Homevisiting: Procedures for helping families. Newbury Park, Califormia: Sage Publications, Inc.

Whitaker, C. & Keith, D. (1981). "Symbolic-experiential family therapy." In D. Gurman & D. Kniskern (Eds.), Handbook of family therapy. New York: Brunner-Mazel.

Whitelaw-Downs, S. (1994). Skillman Center for Children: Neighborhood-based family support. Detroit: Wayne State University, Skillman Center for Children.

Williams, K. R. (1984). Economic sources of homicide: Reestimating the effects of poverty and inequality. American Sociological Review, 49, p. 283-289.

Wilson, L. & Stith, S. (1991). Culturally sensitive therapy with Black clients. Journal of Multicultural Counseling and Development, 19, (1), p. 32-43.

Wolfgang, M. E. & Ferracuti, F. (1967). The subculture of violence. Beverly Hills, Sage Publications.

Woods, M. E. & Hollis, F. (1990). Casework: A psychosocial therapy, fourth edition. New York: McGraw-Hill Publishing Company.

Woodson, C. G. (1972). The history of the Negro church. Washington, D.C.: The Associated Publishers.

Wright, R., Saleby, D., Watts, T. & Lecca, P. (1983). Transcultural perspectives in the human services. Illinois: Charles Thomas.

Yelder, T. (1976). Generational relationships in black families: Some perceptions of grandparents' roles. Unpublished doctoral dissertation, University of Southern California, Los Angleos.

Index

Abuse, 7, 11, 73, 78-83
 physical, 7, 78-83
 sexual, 7, 11, 73, 133-135
Accommodation, 88-91, 91, 97-98
Active listening, 9
 during assessment, 17
Adaptability of family roles, 19-20, 27, 48
Adjustment Disorder, 68-69
 with Depressed mood, 68
Adjustment issues, 97, 122-124
Adolescence, 30-32, 34-40, 76-78
Adoption, 61
Adult Outpatient Services, 66-69
Advocacy
 motherhood
 shortage of marriagable mates
 as heads of households
 marriage
 Women's groups, 45
African American aged, 42, 59-60
African American children, 21-26, 33, 38, 92, 101-105
 socialization, 42
African American Church, 57-63, 94-97, 135-138
 African Methodist Episcapal, 62
 Church of God in Christ, 62
 National Baptist Convention of America, Inc. 62
 National Missionary Baptist Convention of America, 62
 Progressive National Baptist Convention, 62
African American Families
 barriers to services, 91-98
 births, 38
 child-rearing, 42, 92
 children, 1, 19-20, 21-26, 30, 38, 42, 92, 101-105, 133-135

Church, 4, 54, 59-69, 94-97, 137-138
culture, 1, 3, 16
divorce, 38
engagement, 34-37
extended family, 4, 17, 19, 34, 41-56, 138-139
family therapy issues with, 6-7
fathers, 33, 39
female-headed, 38-40, 66-69, 98
gender roles in, 27-40
grandparents as primary caregivers, 11
history, 4-12, 41-56
households,
male and female roles, 27-40
marriage, 39
mothers, 39, 91-98
parenting, 38, 48
pregnancies, 38
research on, 1
roles, 19-20
self-esteem, 4
strategies and techniques for working with, 85-139
strengths, 101-105
African American men, 28-33, 39-40, 73-75
 aggression, 28-31, 74-75
 anger, 29-31, 74-75
 communication, 31
 domestic violence, 73-75
 economics, 32
 education, 28, 32
 endangerment of, 28-29
 engagement, 33-40
 employment, 28
 fathers, 33, 39
 husbands, 39
 male and female relationships, 27

155